C000221244

THE MYSTERY OF
SKARA BRAE

"Antiquarian scholar Laird Scranton has done it again. In his latest book, *The Mystery of Skara Brae,* he takes the reader to one of the most remote locations in the British Isles, then proceeds to lay out the heretofore unknown story of a well-organized yet mysterious culture that flourished off the western coast of Scotland, only to decamp forever around 2600 BCE. Who were the inhabitants of Skara Brae, and what connection did they have with the peoples who went on to create ancient Egypt? What knowledge did they share with the ancient African tribe the Dogon? Where did they come from, and to where did they disappear? Scranton guides us through time and tradition in an account that both novices and scholars will embrace. . . . marvelous and highly educational. I would recommend it unhesitatingly to anyone interested in ancient mysteries."

PETER ROBBINS,
COAUTHOR OF *LEFT AT EAST GATE* AND
AUTHOR OF *DELIBERATE DECEPTION*
AND *HALT IN WOODBRIDGE*

"If you are interested in ancient mysteries, then you must read the writings of Laird Scranton. . . . *The Mystery of Skara Brae* is a welcome addition to his amazing library of work. Connections between ancient cultures that would not seem to be related at first glance have long fascinated me, and no one explores these connections better than Laird, both in his scholarship and level of detail. If you want to explore the evidence on the eerie similarities between ancient civilizations, get your copy of *The Mystery of Skara Brae* today."

JIM HAROLD, HOST OF *THE PARANORMAL PODCAST* AND AUTHOR OF *TRUE GHOST STORIES*—JIM HAROLD'S CAMPFIRE SERIES

THE MYSTERY OF
SKARA BRAE

Neolithic Scotland and the Origins of Ancient Egypt

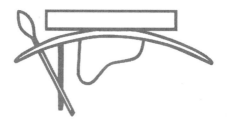

LAIRD SCRANTON

Inner Traditions

Rochester, Vermont • Toronto, Canada

Inner Traditions
One Park Street
Rochester, Vermont 05767
www.InnerTraditions.com

Text stock is SFI certified

Copyright © 2016 by Laird Scranton

All rights reserved. No part of this book may be reproduced or utilized in
any form or by any means, electronic or mechanical, including photocopying,
recording, or by any information storage and retrieval system, without permission
in writing from the publisher.

Library of Congress Cataloging-in-Publication Data
Names: Scranton, Laird, 1953– author.
Title: The mystery of Skara Brae : Neolithic Scotland and the origins of ancient
   Egypt / Laird Scranton.
Description: Rochester, Vermont : Inner Traditions, 2016.
Identifiers: LCCN 2016018651 (print) | LCCN 2016024870 (e-book) |
   ISBN 9781620555736 (paperback) | ISBN 9781620555743 (e-book)
Subjects: LCSH: Skara Brae Site (Scotland) | Neolithic period—Scotland—
   Orkney. | Orkney (Scotland)—Antiquities. | Prehistoric peoples—Scotland—
   Orkney. | Megalithic monuments—Scotland—Orkney. | Göbekli Tepe
   (Turkey) | Dogon (African people)—Mali—Social life and customs. | Egypt—
   Social life and customs—To 332 B.C. | Egypt—Relations—Scotland—Orkney. |
   Orkney (Scotland)—Relations—Egypt. | BISAC: BODY, MIND & SPIRIT /
   Mythical Civilizations. | HISTORY / Ancient / General. | BODY, MIND &
   SPIRIT / Unexplained Phenomena.
Classification: LCC GN776.22.G7 S465 2016 (print) | LCC GN776.22.G7 (e-book) |
   DDC 936.1/132—dc23
LC record available at https://lccn.loc.gov/2016018651

Figures on pages 28 and 119 licensed under Creative Commons 2.0 https://
creativecommons.org/licenses/by/2.0/legalcode
Bottom cover image by Wknight 94 and figure on page 83 licensed under Creative
Commons 3.0 https://creativecommons.org/licenses/bysa/3.0/legalcode

Printed and bound in the United States by Lake Book Manufacturing, Inc.
The text stock is SFI certified. The Sustainable Forestry Initiative® program
promotes sustainable forest management.

10 9 8 7 6 5 4 3 2 1

Text design and layout by Virginia Scott Bowman
This book was typeset in Garmond Premier Pro with Trajan Pro and Avenir used
as display typefaces

To send correspondence to the author of this book, mail a first-class letter to the
author c/o Inner Traditions • Bear & Company, One Park Street, Rochester, VT
05767, and we will forward the communication.

❖ ❖

When they die, hearts that were void of mercy pay the due penalty, and of this world's sins a judge below the earth holds trial, and of dread necessity declares the word of doom. But the good, through the nights alike, and through the days unending, beneath the sun's bright ray, tax not the soil with the strength of their hands, nor the broad sea for a poor living, but enjoy a life that knows no toil; with men honoured of heaven, who kept their sworn word gladly, spending an age free from all tears. But the unjust endure pain that no eye can bear to see. But those who had good courage, three times on either side of death, to keep their hearts untarnished of all wrong, these travel along the road of Zeus to Kronos' tower. There round the Islands of the Blest (Nesoi Makaron), the winds of Okeanos play.

PINDAR, *OLYMPIAN ODE 2*

CONTENTS

INTRODUCTION

Some Thoughts on Comparative Cosmology

My field of study is called comparative cosmology. Most simply, this means that I compare the similar symbols, words, concepts, rituals, and deities of ancient cultures in the hope of learning more about them. Ancient cosmology is a field of study that, more than many others, is founded on inherent uncertainties. As any good criminal investigator eventually discovers, first and foremost among these are the uncertainties of eyewitness testimony, which is what many historical accounts effectively represent. Any researcher of ancient culture understands before he or she even begins work that his or her chosen field rests on a foundation of incomplete knowledge, often made even more uncertain by the compounding distortions of interpretation and entrenched theory.

Added to these are the uncertainties of an inexplicable phenomenon I call *informed blindness*—situations in which a person's own preconceptions induce him or her to look past significant facts. As an example of this phenomenon, I ask myself, how is it possible that Egyptologists, over the course of two centuries, never noticed that the glyphs of the Egyptian word for "week" symbolically defined the Egyptian concept of a week? Likewise, for more than six decades, how could researchers of Dogon culture not have recognized the Dogon granary as a form of a Buddhist stupa? Myself having occasionally been subject to this same

1

inexplicable inability to see what is flatly before my eyes, I understand that this phenomenon might simply be an unavoidable circumstance of cognition and pursuit of a working theory—something that unfathomably just happens.

The main goal of a comparative cosmologist is to increase the value of this uncertain body of knowledge by using powers of comparison. We know that the net benefit of comparing two versions of a myth or symbol is akin to scanning an image with two eyes, rather than just one. What is ultimately gained by doing so is an improved sense of perspective.

There are five previous volumes in this series on ancient cosmology and language. These include *The Science of the Dogon, Sacred Symbols of the Dogon, The Cosmological Origins of Myth and Symbol, China's Cosmological Prehistory,* and *Point of Origin.* While there will be references in this book to concepts, facts, and ideas that may have been discussed in greater detail in these prior volumes, there is no expectation that the reader will have read them as a prerequisite to understanding what is presented here. Although this book is the fifth in that series, it represents a first deliberate attempt to uncover information about an ancient society based not on clear statements made within that culture itself, but rather by comparison of what we know about that society with facts that have been previously correlated for other cultures. In this volume our focus is on the Orkney Islands, which lie just to the north of Scotland. This is a region of the world that is distantly removed from Africa and Asia, where our previous research has largely centered. More specifically, we will be discussing the coastal village of Skara Brae, a small Neolithic farming settlement whose prehistoric lifestyle and traditions are poorly understood by modern researchers.

We begin this effort not with the kind of carefully preserved oral tradition that researchers encountered among the Dogon priests, nor with a body of inscriptions, written texts, and artwork such as are found from ancient Egypt, but rather with a single motivating question to explore (i.e., whether Egyptian influences might have been at work at

Skara Brae), a somewhat sparse set of excavated ruins, a handful of enigmatic stone structures, and a limited collection of poorly understood artifacts. The truth is that researchers on the scene do not yet know who founded the village, have no working theory of where the earliest inhabitants of the island came from, consider certain stylistic elements of construction and pottery in the village to be unique, and deem the language spoken there to be of uncertain origin. Framed in these ways, we can scarcely say that the focus of our project sounds particularly promising.

Among the special tools we bring to bear on this study is an overview of symbolic systems from a broad range of ancient cultures. These are rooted in an understanding of the instructive cosmology of the modern-day Dogon tribe of Mali, in northwest Africa, which exists as a kind of crossroads for several ancient traditions. The Dogon priests retain a clear sense of their own ancient tradition and are able to explain its elements in modern terms. Our previous studies have armed us with a set of correlated terms of cosmology whose meanings we can understand and whose permutations of pronunciation and usage will become familiar to us. Also at our disposal is an Egyptian hieroglyphic dictionary, whose words will provide us with unique insights into the intended meanings of a wide range of ancient cosmological terms.

Several of our previous studies have focused on societies who managed to retain a high degree of purity of language. This is particularly true of the Dogon, who as a culture prioritize the ancient meanings of symbols, words, and ritual practices, and who hand them down carefully from generation to generation. In the case of ancient Egypt, we have inscriptions that were literally carved in stone, and so preserved the precise written forms of words as they appeared to the Egyptians many thousands of years ago. We also have explored and positively correlated an extensive set of Dogon words to matching Egyptian word forms in our previous studies, and we have thereby gained perspective on the pronunciation and meanings of a large body of ancient words.

However, this is not the case with Skara Brae, whose structures predated the onset of written language in most cultures. Here we have no excavated texts to use as a guide or to give us a frame of reference. Furthermore, in the case of Skara Brae, words of various modern Scandinavian languages have intermingled somewhat indiscriminately with ancient ones for more than 4,600 years, often obscuring any original sense of meaning. So we begin our study with no guarantees that the ancient word forms we seek to compare may have even managed to survive within the language.

One beneficial effect that works in our favor when studying these languages is a linguistic phenomenon called *ultraconserved words*. This term refers to the tendency of significant words of a culture to remain in a language for very long periods of time. Fortunately for our studies, later cultures often revere ancient cosmological words, so traces of the words' original pronunciations and meanings often remain in evidence.

Another great advantage we bring to this study is a unique perspective on how the ancient traditions of Africa, Egypt, India, Tibet, and China related to one another. In our view, these cultures shared a common originating source at around 10,000 BCE and a lineage that links forward through an archaic tradition in India called the Sakti cult, whose modern-day center of observance is located in a region of southeast India called Orissa. From an Indian perspective, this cult had its origins in the northwest mountains of India, in the same general region as the Fertile Crescent, and these origins are understood to reach back in time to a period long before the advent of writing. Iconic elements of the Sakti tradition are in evidence at the archaic megalithic sanctuary of Gobekli Tepe in Turkey, which is thought to be nearly twelve thousand years old. Many of these same elements are also found in ancient Turkish cosmology and among the Dravidians, and are known to be ancestral to the Vedic tradition, Buddhism, and Hinduism. In *Point of Origin* we argued that these same elements also link credibly forward through the Sakti cult to predynastic Egypt and later on to the Dogon in northwest Africa. Signature elements of the tradition are also found in ancient Tibet and China and seem to have been transmitted from there into North America. The process of tracing this cosmology down through the millennia has touched on many of the most common permutations of the tradition, which gives us some added perspective on which cosmological forms we might expect to find in context with which others.

Each regional culture also brings its own set of languages to bear on the symbols and concepts we explore. These include the Dogon language, whose cosmological words are essentially Egyptian; the Tamil language of the Dravidians, many of whose words also entered the Dogon language; the Turkish language; the Egyptian hieroglyphic language; and the Dongba language of the Na-Khi tribe in Tibet. We have demonstrated that various cosmological terms of China are often also recognizable variants of Dogon and Egyptian words. We have also been able to correlate key cosmological concepts of India, which are expressed in the phonetically different language of Sanskrit, to matching Dogon and Egyptian concepts.

The field of ancient studies is an arena in which absolute proof of an observation or interpretation may not always be possible. For that reason, our emphasis has been primarily on demonstrating points, not proving them. Many times these demonstrations take the form of direct side-by-side comparisons, in which two symbols, words, concepts, definitions, or images that are in some way intuitively similar to one another are set side by side so that the readers may simply perceive a match for themselves.

In the field of ancient studies, inference can also greatly increase the value of any simple fact we may uncover. A fact tells us what a thing is, while inferences can open other potentially important doors for us. For example, one discrete fact we can point to is that around 400 BCE the Buddhists documented a system of cosmology that is a match for the modern Dogon tradition, and so suggests that the Dogon system must also be at least that old. However, a powerful inference we can draw from this fact is that, in order for the two systems to still match, neither can have changed substantially over the course of nearly 2,500 years.

Some readers who may be new to ancient cosmology might see it as a complex or somewhat intimidating subject and might worry that a prior background in the subject could be required in order to understand what is presented here. Hopefully that will not be the case. Whenever issues of cosmology become pertinent in these chapters, the intention is to provide as direct an explanation as possible for the benefit of those who may not be familiar with the terms or concepts involved.

1

A Brief History of Skara Brae

Skara Brae is the name of a small prehistoric village located along the west shore of Orkney Island, or Mainland, which is the largest island in the Orkney Islands archipelago, situated just to the north of Scotland. The village is scenically set, overlooking a brilliant white beach that runs along the Bay of Skaill. Archaeological dating techniques suggest that the village was originally settled during Neolithic times, sometime after 3200 BCE, and may have been inhabited by as many as twenty families for a period of more than six hundred years, up until around 2500 BCE.[1] After that time, for reasons unknown, the village was apparently abandoned, its buildings then covered over with sand and mud, at least partly by natural forces. From the perspective of modern historians, this seemingly unintended burial turns out to have been a fortuitous circumstance, since it effectively protected and preserved the major features of the village. Thereafter, Skara Brae sat silently entombed just beneath the surface, and so it remained completely unknown to later culture for more than forty centuries.

During the winter of 1850, a series of violent storms struck the island and partially exposed a portion of the village that lay on a high dune owned by William Watt, the Laird of Skaill. Watt, who lived only a short distance from the site, recognized the unique nature and historical importance of what had been uncovered and over the next eight years made efforts to begin excavating and preserving it.

7

Professional excavations were also later conducted at the Skara Brae site. The first of these, from 1928 through 1930, was overseen by V. Gordon Childe, a professor of British prehistory, and consultations were made with such authorities as Sir William Matthew Flinders Petrie, who was known for his studies of ancient Egypt. A third excavation was undertaken in more recent times, more than forty years later, in 1972 and 1973. These later efforts located several additional structures not originally brought to light by Watt.[2]

Although Skara Brae overlooks the sea in the present day, some researchers believe that the site may have originally been set farther back from the sea, perhaps next to a freshwater lagoon separated from the beach by dunes. From their perspective, encroaching sea levels would have changed the apparent location of the village over time by bringing the sea's edge somewhat closer to it.[3]

Because the village of Skara Brae was built before the advent of written historical records, there is little that can be said with certainty about its inhabitants, what their daily life was like, or from where they may have originally come. Based on surviving evidence, it can be inferred that they were skilled farmers who made good use of the fertile land and hospitable climate of the Orkney Islands. Orkney Island is situated as far north in latitude as Hudson's Bay, but because of warm ocean currents that circulate along the coast, the weather on Orkney Island is more temperate, and so more hospitable to farming.

Orkney Island is believed to have been inhabited since around 3700 BCE, and the earliest settlements are thought to have taken the form of single-family farms, consisting of only one or two buildings. Several archaic family farm sites have been excavated in the region. The settlement at Skara Brae demonstrates that by around 3100 BCE, people there had begun to establish small farming communities. Well-preserved features of Skara Brae offer us some direct insight into what the daily life of its residents may have been like. Significantly, no weapons or fortifications have been uncovered among the artifacts at

Skara Brae, which suggests that the life there must have been a peaceful one. All indications are that the site represented a simple farming village.

The careful stonework that was revealed in the excavated Skara Brae structures gives clear testimony to the stone-working skills of the inhabitants of the village. Stone was plentiful on the island and was of a type that could be easily broken or cut into regular pieces suitable for use in construction. These stones lent themselves to dry-wall construction, where flat rocks are simply stacked and offset with one another without mortar to form walls. The earliest stone walls at Skara Brae were freestanding, but later ones were insulated and supported on one side by earthen mounds formed essentially from compost heaps comprised of waste that was left over from various daily activities. Materials found in these mounds provide archaeologists with important clues about how the villagers lived.

Trees were scarce on the island, and any wood that was available for construction consisted mostly of driftwood that washed up on the shores of the island. However, artifacts show that the people of Skara Brae made effective use of the various materials they did have at hand, such as stone, bone, and clay, to establish and sustain a comparatively high quality of life in the village.

Each of the original houses at Skara Brae was built on essentially the same basic plan, one whose central focus was a square room with rounded corners, with rectangular alcoves on each side that were used for storage. In the middle of the floor of the house was a flat, square stone hearth. Toward the front of the house, the plan often included a small, round, beehive-shaped cell, described by researchers as a "unique" architectural feature and interpreted by some to have been a latrine. The houses also featured two bed platforms set along the walls on either side of the hearth. These were situated behind a standing slab of stone that absorbed heat from the fire, prevented the fire's light from shining directly in the eyes of a sleeping person, and made the bed platform warmer. It is presumed that soft materials such as bracken, heather, and animal skins were placed in these partitioned platforms to make them into comfortable sleeping surfaces.[4]

Skara Brae was actually built twice during the course of its lifetime, in many cases with new structures raised directly over the top of prior ones, perhaps due to lack of available space. Therefore, most of what remains today is representative of the later, rebuilt village. The only original structures visible today are those that were not covered over by newer ones.

Food appears to have been in ample supply at Skara Brae. In addition to the farming of grains like barley, the people there raised cattle and sheep. They also gathered eggs from seafowl and hunted deer for meat. It is presumed that they fished, although no obvious fishing equipment or accessories such as hooks have been found during the excavations. It is surmised by some researchers that the square watertight boxes that are often found on the floors of Skara Brae houses were designed to hold limpets, to be used as fish bait.[5]

In ancient times, Orkney Island was known in Scandinavia by the name Orkneyar or Orknejar. Another ancient name for the island is given as Argat.[6] The island is known to have been host to at least two distinct cultural groups who are mentioned in Scandinavian sagas. The first was a group of likely indigenous pygmies "of strange habits," referred to as the Peti. In ancient times, the islands were called *terra Petorum,* or land of the Peti. The second was a people who are described as having dressed in white cloaks like clerics, known as the Papae, a term that was generally applied to all clerics.[7] One local language of Orkney Island defines the word *papi* to mean "father."[8]

As we might expect given the existence of two distinct groups in the region, two archaic languages are also known to have existed on Orkney Island. The first, called Norn, is closely related to Norwegian. The second, called Faroese (a name taken from the same root as the name of the nearby Faroe Islands), is, like the Papae clerics, of unknown origin and not obviously founded on Scandinavian roots.

As also might be expected in a case such as this one where there are no written records to refer to as documentation, a wide range of opinions exists as to who the Neolithic farmers of Skara Brae might have been and where they originally came from. In the more academically traditional theories, the candidates have ranged from the Picts to the Phoenicians, while the perhaps more speculative ones look to such wide-ranging groups as the Atlanteans.

2

Footholds to a Theory of Origin for Skara Brae

Since my personal background as an author is that of a comparative cosmologist, this means that for twenty years or more I have compared the words, symbols, myths, and rituals of ancient cultures. Over the years I have researched and written about cultures from Africa, Egypt, India, Tibet, China, and Polynesia, correlating and comparing numerous aspects of these ancient cultures during various historical and prehistoric eras.

My studies began in the mid-1990s with a little-known African tribe from Mali called the Dogon. The Dogon tribe was of interest because their culture presents a kind of crossroads for several ancient traditions. The Dogon are a priestly tribe who place a very high value on the purity of words and rituals. Although some of their practices are arguably more than five thousand years old, the Dogon priests still understand and can clearly explain the rationale behind their long-held concepts and societal practices. Dogon religious rituals are like those of ancient Judaism, their civic traditions are consistently similar to those of ancient Egypt, and their system of cosmology is a point-for-point match for an ancient Buddhist cosmology associated with a ritual shrine called a stupa, which like ancient shrines of many cultures was ritually aligned to the cardinal points of north, south, east, and west. Moreover, the Dogon tradition is defined by what are arguably ancient Egyptian words and symbolic shapes that are set down by the Dogon priests as cosmological drawings. These broad, cross-societal resemblances offer new opportunities to compare symbolic definitions and practices between cultures. The many similarities and differences that arise from these comparisons open new windows into what various rituals and practices may have meant to the ancient cultures who observed them.

The Dogon are known for their careful devotion to maintaining the purity of language and rituals. Evidence of this is seen in the very close match that can be shown to exist between their system of cosmology and the Buddhist cosmology. Sadly, the same cannot be said for most cultures, so our expectation is that, over time, influences from other cultures or languages are likely to have been introduced that may interfere with our ability to make direct comparisons between words or meanings.

One important aspect of these comparisons is that they enable us to place these practices into a historical time line or framework. For example, the many words and traditions shared commonly by the Dogon and the ancient Egyptians suggest that the two cultures must have had a long period of intimate contact with one another during some ancient era. By comparing aspects of Dogon culture to those known to have existed at various points in Egyptian culture, we can set reasoned limits on the historical epoch in which that contact is likeliest to have occurred.

For example, we know that written language made its first appearance in ancient Egypt at or around 3000 BCE. The absence of a written language among the Dogon suggests that any prolonged contact they may have had with the Egyptians must have happened sometime prior to that era. We also know that the Dogon observe the same diverse set of solar, lunar, agricultural, and civic calendars as the ancient Egyptians. However, the Dogon practice does not include the system of five intercalary days (five leap-year days) that is known to have been adopted by the Egyptians by around 2900 BCE to reconcile their calendars. This cultural difference would again suggest that any period of close contact between the Dogon and Egyptians must have taken place prior to that time, circa 3000 BCE. Other similar comparisons can be made between the Dogon and the predynastic and/or dynastic Egyptians that confirm this same time frame as the likeliest era of contact between the two groups.

Using comparisons like these, as we set effective limits on when certain practices were likely to have appeared or been in use, we build a kind of conceptual time line for ourselves to illustrate when certain practices emerged in relation to others. For example, along this time line, we know that stone cairns appeared before aligned ritual shrines, and that both cairns and aligned shrines appeared before mastabas or pyramids. We also know that the various conceptual elements of the zodiac seem to have existed from archaic times, but that a properly formulated zodiac did not finally take form until around 700 BCE. This kind of relational framework for the various historical elements allows us to estimate time frames whenever we encounter similar elements in other ancient cultures.

The Dogon are the keepers of an extensive creation tradition that defines, in remarkably scientific terms, how the universe formed, how matter is created, and how biological reproduction happens. Daily life in Dogon society is intimately interconnected with important aspects of their creation tradition, so there is a cosmological rationale that underlies most aspects of Dogon life. Many of the structures of their society reflect important themes and concepts of their creation tradition, which serve to reinforce those concepts for tribe members. For example, the archaic method by which Dogon farmers plowed their fields was meant to reflect an important process in the formation of matter. In similar ways, other Dogon practices were formulated to reflect various concepts central to their creation tradition.

Consider the following as a practical example of how cosmology intertwines with Dogon life: The Dogon approach to organizing their agricultural fields centers on a theoretical concept called the well-field system. This system is based on a three-by-three grid of plots, consisting of nine squares of land, each measuring eight cubits per side. Eight of these plots surround a ninth plot that is meant to hold a central, commonly shared well (from which the term *well-field* derives). Eight families work and benefit from the produce of the eight outer plots, while cooperatively sharing the well. Each of the component elements that make up this system (the conception of land in squares, the cubit as a unit of measure, the choice to define the system in terms of eight families, the sum of three plots and twenty-four cubits per side of the grid, and so on) has its basis in an underlying system of cosmology. The apparent intention was that the structures of daily life, formulated in this way on creational concepts, would help preserve and transmit cosmological meaning from generation to generation. So later, when we encounter this same well-field system described as the theoretical basis of land management in ancient China, we recognize immediately that it must reflect the influence of this same system of cosmology.

To me, the job of a comparative cosmologist is not unlike that of a police investigator who interviews potential suspects in a murder case. The questions we ask are intended to distinguish actual suspects from apparent ones by essentially ruling out all but the real perpetrators. Sometimes this can be done on the basis of a single contradictory fact. If a potential suspect can show that he or she was seen attending a dinner party at the time the murder was committed, then that person cannot reasonably have committed the murder and so should no longer be considered a suspect. To quote Sherlock Holmes, "When you have eliminated the impossible, whatever remains, however improbable, must be the truth."

My introduction to the mysteries of Skara Brae came about when an acquaintance of mine named Andy Monk asked if I thought that the ancient Egyptians could have been involved in the settlement there. My first impulse when presented with a question of this type (especially one that may step outside of my immediate areas of knowledge) is to look for some outward factor on which the question might turn. Many times the most immediate solution to a problem involves some detail that either directly supports or flatly contradicts the premise of the question.

Knowing that the artifacts from Skara Brae date from the same approximate time period as I place Dogon involvement with the Egyptians, and knowing what a superb job the Dogon have done preserving their words and traditions down through the ages, it occurred to me that if the founding residents of Skara Brae had actually been Egyptian, then I might expect to find commonalities between the lifestyle at Skara Brae and modern Dogon life. Taking this as the initial thrust of my approach, I effectively transformed the question from one that I might not be entirely equipped to answer ("Were the people at Skara Brae Egyptians?") to one that I felt eminently qualified to explore ("In what ways do the lifestyle and ritual life at Skara Brae resemble those of the Dogon?").

3
REEXAMINING SKARA
BRAE IN OVERVIEW

When approaching comparative questions of lifestyle at Skara Brae, it seems fortuitous that most aspects of Dogon life rest on an explicit rationale. In other words, there is a reason why they do things, and even after the passage of many centuries, the Dogon priests clearly understand that rationale. Nearly every aspect of Dogon life has assigned symbolism. Knowing this adds another dimension to our discussion of Skara Brae, one in which we can ask whether the well-defined Dogon rationale fits what we see in the Skara Brae village.

One sensible point at which to begin our exploration of the question of possible Egyptian involvement at Skara Brae would seem to be the general attributes of the village itself. There are numerous sources, written by people who are familiar with the excavations at Skara Brae, that describe these attributes. Another starting point would lie with the earliest historical descriptions we have of the peoples who were found to natively inhabit Orkney Island, given by early chroniclers from Scandinavia. These early sagas devote scant attention to describing the natives of the island, other than to simply delineate the two distinct groups of pygmies and clerics, the Peti and Papae, respectively. Yet another potential source for insight into the possible origins of the Orkney Island population is found in recent DNA studies that have been carried out in the region.

The first and perhaps most obvious question to ask in any comparison

The Neolithic village site at Skara Brae on Orkney Island as currently reconstructed. Photo by Isaac Scranton.

of Skara Brae with Dogon domiciles is whether the excavated remains at Skara Brae bear any outward resemblances to a Dogon village. For me, the immediate answer to that question lies not with words but with images. Allowing for the fact that the Skara Brae researchers could only speculate about what roofing materials might have been used and so were unable to accurately reconstruct the roofs of structures as they originally appeared, compare this overview of the reconstructed Skara Brae site (below) with this similarly framed overview of a modern-day Dogon village on page 19.

A person could argue that structures built from stone by any two cultures might tend to resemble one another simply due to the nature of the building material. However, in each of these cases there are certain design choices to be considered that can be positively compared. In the case of these two overview images, it seems easy to perceive the villages as falling along a single architectural continuum. For example, both plans give preference to and demonstrate comparable skill at dry-wall

A modern-day Dogon village in Africa. Photo by Dewey Webster,
www.deweywebster.net/dogon.html.

construction. One obvious feature that the villages share in common
with one another is the architectural choice to define a protected inner
passageway between the buildings of the village.

We understand that differences in climate impose certain choices
when it comes to the construction of a village. For example, the Dogon
live in a desert region that sees little rain and so are able to use mud as
a material to construct many of their buildings, since dried mud, which
remains dry in a desert climate, retains its structural integrity. Likewise,
wood is in greater supply in Dogon country than it was on Orkney
Island and so is more accessible as a building material. The noticeably
colder climate of Northern Scotland compelled the people at Skara Brae
to build thicker walls and to insulate their walls on the outer side with
midden, neither of which the Dogon climate would require.

Notwithstanding those considerations, there is similarity in the way
that squared structures of the two villages are interspersed with rounded
ones, and there is a similar flow to the relative placement of buildings
and open spaces in each village. The heights of the freestanding walls

are comparable to one another in both villages. The relationship of wall height to the heights of buildings is comparable. The widths of the internal passageways are comparable. From the perspective of our comparisons, there would seem to be no compelling reason to argue that the two villages must have come out of different traditions. On the contrary, based solely on outward appearances it seems thinkable that they might well have come out of the same tradition.

Perhaps the next most obvious question to be asked is whether the very limited descriptions we have of the earliest inhabitants of Skara Brae and the Orkney region could apply to (or might possibly rule out) Egyptians cast in a somewhat earlier mode, similar to what the Dogon now represent. The notion of an early group on Orkney Island characterized as clerics is actually a good match for the Dogon, who even today are described as a "priestly" tribe. We know that descriptions of these Orkney Island clerics as being clad in white cloaks is also a good match for traditional images of the Dogon, who are often pictured dressed in white. The French anthropologist Genevieve Calame-Griaule describes a white tunic as the traditional garb of the tribe. The ancient Scandinavian term applied to these clerics, Papae, could also make sense in relation to Dogon cosmology, which is founded on a creational concept of matter called *po* or *pau*, which is rendered in some cultures as *pa*. The Dogon word *pa* means "age."[1] According to Sir E. A. Wallis Budge, author of *An Egyptian Hieroglyphic Dictionary,* the Egyptian word *pa* also meant "ancestor," a term that the Dogon assign to their mythical bringers of civilizing skills.[2] Given the relationship of Egyptian cosmology to later cultures and religions, it seems possible that this same essential phoneme might have survived in our own culture in the term *pagan*.

From the perspective of overview, we also know that the Skara Brae settlers demonstrated the abilities of experienced farmers, herders, and hunters. These are skills that are also overtly exhibited by both the Dogon and the ancient Egyptians. The blind Dogon priest Ogotemmeli, who served as a primary consultant to anthropologists when they were documenting Dogon cosmology, had been an accomplished hunter. But the way in which all these skills were integrated at Skara Brae seems somewhat remarkable to researchers familiar with Neolithic life in the Orkney Islands. One BBC commentator stated, "Such a tightly knit and communal village life was unusual in these early farming communities, individual farmsteads being preferred, but Skara Brae seems to have been a very close community with little room for non-conformists."[3]

By contrast, these very same features that seem aberrant and somewhat out of place in the context of Orkney Island can be said to be absolutely characteristic of the Dogon village life, where closeness, peaceful cooperation, consistency, and tradition are among the everyday attributes of what can only be called an exceedingly stable cultural tradition. Most researchers recognize a similar kind of societal stability to have been a hallmark of life in ancient Egypt, a culture that survived and held many of its cultural forms for nearly three thousand years.

Our third potential entry point to the possible identities of the inhabitants of Skara Brae comes from consideration of their genetic heritage. The Faroe Island region has been the focus of recent DNA studies that, not surprisingly, reveal strong Scandinavian influences in the DNA of inhabitants there. The mere similarities of the Norn language to modern Norwegian suggest that would be the case. However, the studies also reveal an intermix of DNA types from a variety of different cultures, characterized by researchers as indicating "high levels of genetic drift" among the Orkney Island population. Some of the genetic influences cited for Orkney Island in a 2012 study include DNA markers from North Africa, which are attributed, for reasons not expressly outlined, to interaction with Barbary pirates in the 1700s. No statement is made (nor after thousands of years might any coherent statement really be practical) regarding any potentially ancient influences from Africa on the populace on Orkney Island.

More difficult to explain is the presence of a yDNA haplogroup that is widely present in modern Egyptian men and among men of

Scandinavia and the Faroe Islands. Because the Y chromosomes pass from father to son almost unchanged, they can be quite useful and dependable in tracking the genealogy of a person or a group of people. DNA studies have shown that the Dogon share this same genetic marker with the Berbers (predynastic Egyptian) and Tuareg people from northern Africa. And recent studies also show that 1 percent of the male population in the Faroe Islands share these same markers.[4]

Author Alistair Moffatt, who has written about recent DNA studies in the region of Scotland, describes it as "one of the most diverse nations on earth," citing findings there of West African, Arabian, Southeast Asian, and Siberian ancestry.[5] Based on those results, questions could be reasonably raised as to how Egyptian and North African DNA might have made its way to Scandinavia.

We understand that there may be no way to distinguish DNA that was acquired by a populace in ancient times from DNA that entered the gene pool in more recent times. Although we know that these findings alone cannot definitively demonstrate either an Egyptian or an otherwise African presence in the region of Northern Scotland at 3200 BCE, the significant detection of these markers does disallow us from flatly ruling it out.[6]

4

Comparing Skara Brae and Dogon Structures

As we continue to pursue the question of how lifestyle and ritual life at Skara Brae resembled those of the Dogon, our next likely step would be to select individual structures found at Skara Brae and compare their features to similar Dogon forms. What we would hope to consider in these comparisons is the architectural layout of structures, the method of construction used, the relative dimensions of structural features, any unique structural features that may be exhibited, and any symbolism that relates to those structures and features.

Since researchers say that the earliest living spaces at Skara Brae follow a basic pattern and we also know that Dogon stone houses are typically built to a predefined plan, it only makes sense to compare various elements of those plans.

Olivier Dunrea's book *Skara Brae: The Story of a Prehistoric Village* is presented in the form of a children's book, but it gives a good (if partially fictionalized) overview of the history of the site. It is offered as a description of what life may have been like at Skara Brae, based on the assumptions of researchers who have studied the site. Specific details about the life of the village have been inferred from the types of artifacts found there and through comparison to traditions that were observed later on Orkney Island.

It is particularly helpful to our purposes that the book includes a detailed plan for one of the early houses built at Skara Brae (see image on next page).[1]

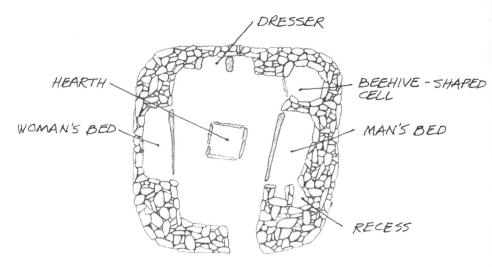

Plan of Skara Brae house. Illustration by Olivier Dunrea from Skara Brae: The Story of a Prehistoric Village.

The plan centers on a square hearth, set out on the floor of the house with stones to define its border. Stone bed platforms are built into recesses along two opposing walls on either side of the hearth, with the doorway or entry to the house located in the center of a third wall. The fourth wall holds a built-in dresser and leads to an unusual feature situated in the furthest right corner of the house: a round alcove described as a "beehive-shaped cell."

Compare those structural elements at Skara Brae with the plan of a typical Dogon house (opposite page).

In the broadest strokes, we can see that there are several immediate outward similarities between the layouts of the house at Skara Brae and the comparable Dogon house. The first and most obvious is the presence of a very similar circular "beehive-shaped cell" at the head of the Dogon house. Both homes are windowless. For the Dogon, who have been heard to say that if they want light, they can go outside, this is seen as a societal preference. Like the Skara Brae house, the Dogon plan calls for two rectangular alcoves on parallel walls at either side of the structure. Because the Dogon live in a desert climate, the Dogon house has

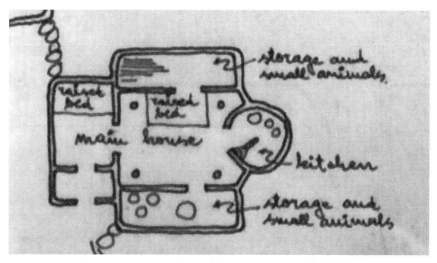

Plan of a Dogon house. From 6,000 Years of Housing, *by Norbert Schoenauer. Used by permission of W. W. Norton.*

little need for a central hearth to warm its residents, and we see none in the plan. However, Dogon hearths situated in open-sided buildings or in uncovered spaces often take this same squared shape and are defined in a similar way with stones that rim the hearth. The floor plan of the Dogon house includes a rectangular inset bed space, not unlike what we see at Skara Brae, and an inside doorway situated in the center of the fourth wall, comparable to its positioning in the Skara Brae house.

Although we have little information to work with when it comes to the house plan at Skara Brae, in the case of the Dogon house we have specific definitions from the Dogon priests regarding an underlying cosmological rationale for its overall plan. Readers who are familiar with the work of R. A. Schwaller de Lubicz, often called the first Egyptian symbolist, may recall his interpretations of the Egyptian Temple of Man, which he felt was constructed to reflect the component structures of a human body. According to the Dogon priests, the same is true for the plan of a Dogon house. The Dogon symbolism is said to be given in relation to the body of a woman. The round "beehive-shaped cell" at the conceptual "top" of the plan is symbolic of the woman's head. The parallel rectangular alcoves on either side of the house define the shoulders and arms of our conceptual woman. The central living space represents the main body cavity. The entryway represented her sexual parts.

The doorway of the Dogon house provides us with both linguistic and symbolic parallels to the house at Skara Brae. The Egyptian term for "door," "doorway," or "threshold" is *hetgat,* or literally "house gate."[2] In the Faroese language of Orkney the term for "doorway" or "threshold" is *gatt.*[3] The Dogon phoneme *ga* means "to depart."[4] Both the Dogon and Faroese words carry a second set of connotations that refer to a person's bodily orifices. In the prior volume of this series, *Point of Origin,* we related the Dogon term *ga* to gateways that are said to exist between stages in the formation of matter and that in India define the elephant god Ganesha, who, in myth, served as the gatekeeper for his mother Sati.

Based on these parallels, we might infer that the plan of the house at Skara Brae reflects the same symbolism that is inherent in the house plan of the Dogon. This symbolism is supported by multiple matched meanings of the similar Faroese, Dogon, and Egyptian words for "doorway" or "threshold." Even features of the Skara Brae house that have no matching correlate in the Dogon plan still seem to conform to the underlying cosmological scenario we think is at play, since the hearth sits where its very name suggests it should sit, in symbolic representation of the heart of the body. In support of this outlook on the symbolism of the Skara Brae house, the Faroese term for "bed" is *flis,*[5] while the word for "arms" is *filio.*[6] One Egyptian word for "heart" is *het,*[7] and the phonetic root of an Egyptian word for "burn" is *heta.*[8]

From the perspective of the Dogon house model, the round "beehive-shaped cell" represents the head of the body and serves as the kitchen. Appropriately, the Dogon word for the "head" on a body is *ku,* while the Faroese term for "kitchen" is *kokur.* The Dogon word for "cook" is *siri,* while the word for "head/chief" is *seru.*[9] (One subtle suggestion of the Dogon double meanings may be that the person who cooks for a household is also effectively in charge of it.) By comparison, the Faroese word for "chief" is *stjori.*

The parallels between the Dogon house and the house at Skara Brae arguably include matching architectural plans, matching construction styles and methods, matching linguistic supports, and matching cosmological schemes, and so they could represent specifically matched symbolic structures. By any reasonable standard, the details of this one building alone could be said to be sufficient to demonstrate a Dogon-style Egyptian influence at Skara Brae. At minimum, it justifies the pursuit of other Dogon or Egyptian linguistic and symbolic parallels in the Orkney region.

The next structure from Skara Brae for our consideration is a round building that takes a markedly different form from the plan of the houses we have just discussed. Compare the images of the Skara Brae structure below to the image of the Dogon structure on page 28.

Two views of round structures at Skara Brae on Orkney Island.
Photos by Isaac Scranton.

In Africa, a Dogon toguna, which is a men's "discussion house"
where disputes are peacefully resolved. Photo: upyernoz from Haverford USA,
uploaded by Albert Herring, cc by-sa 2.0.

Outwardly, we can see that the two structures seem almost identical and exhibit styles of construction that present a very close match for one another. The relative size, dimensions, and structures of the buildings overall, and of the two doorways, are very similar, as is the overall impression they give.

From the perspective of the Dogon, this building represents a *toguna,* or men's discussion house, and is invariably a feature of every Dogon village. In Dogon culture, any interpersonal dispute that might arise is resolved immediately. All interested parties are brought to the discussion house and are required to stay there until the concerns of every participant have been resolved and the issues reconciled. A toguna can be constructed in an open style, in which four pillars built from stones support a pavilion-style roof without walls, or it can be built in a closed style, as shown in the photo. Once again, simple differences in climate might dictate the choice of which form is built.

The Dogon word *toguna* has a likely correlate in the Faroese language that was pronounced *togn.* Among the meanings defined for the Faroese word are "allay," "pacify," "quieten," and "appease." The same term also defines the Faroese concept of peace.[10] In the broader view of the cosmologies we study, the word *togu* means "shelter," while the phoneme *na* refers to the concept of a mother. For example, Tana Penu is the earth mother of the Sakti cult in India, and Nana is the name given to the Neith-like spider mother of the Dogon tradition who weaves matter. From that perspective, we could say that the Dogon succeed in maintaining tranquility in their villages by falling back on a time-honored threat: behave nicely, or we'll take you back to Mom's house.

A Dogon toguna is traditionally built only to half-height, so that those involved in a dispute are compelled to sit down for their discussions—a choice that might tend to reduce tensions and discourage needless fights. In relation to Dogon society, the concept of the toguna arguably makes a significant contribution to the tranquility of a Dogon village. The suggestion is that a similar tradition may have contributed to the apparently peaceful atmosphere at Skara Brae.

5

DOGON, EGYPTIAN, AND FAROESE WORDS OF COSMOLOGY

Another reasonable test of possible Egyptian influence on Orkney Island in ancient times lies with terms that define cosmological concepts. Because these kinds of words lay a conceptual foundation for the ancient religious traditions in which they are found, they tend to fall into the linguistic category of *ultraconserved words*—words that tend to hold their form and meaning within a language for very long periods of time, as noted in the introduction. A significant aspect of the work I have done in comparative cosmology has been to identify and correlate these kinds of words among the various cultures I study. Their significance is such that the ability to demonstrate their presence in the language of an ancient culture constitutes one key test of the cosmology's influence on that culture.

Central to the concepts of Dogon cosmology are definitions of how their tribal god Amma created matter. These descriptions focus significantly on the formation of an underlying structure the Dogon priests call the *po pilu*, or egg of the world. As they describe it, the egg of the world represents the first completed subunit of matter, one that serves as the foundation of a larger atom-like structure called the *po*. The po pilu is the product of seven vibrations of matter, conceived of as seven arrow-like rays of a star of increasing length that radiate outward from a central point or hub, wrapped up and encapsulated inside a kind of primordial egg or bubble. From an alternate perspective, the po pilu is characterized by the spiral that can be drawn to inscribe the endpoints of these rays. The seventh of these rays is said to grow long enough to pierce the egg and actually burst it, an event that is treated as an eighth conceptual stage in the formation of the egg. At the same time, the event also initiates the formation of a new egg.

In the Dogon conception, matter begins in a perfectly ordered state in the form of primordial waves. For the Dogon, existence takes its true form as waves, and our material world represents only a kind of reflected image of that more fundamental wavelike reality. The Dogon and Egyptians define this water-like source of matter with the term *nu*. So it is significant that the Faroese definition of the word *nu* also includes the meanings of "fountain," "spring," and "fountainhead" because it demonstrates that the people at Skara Brae likely understood the cosmological concept of nu in the same essential ways as the Dogon and the Egyptians.[1]

For the Dogon, the processes of creation begin when matter in its wavelike state is disrupted by an act of perception. The Dogon and Egyptians refer to this act using the term *maa*. A comparable Faroese term is the word *møta* (pronounced something akin to *mata*), meaning "see," "discern," "behold," "distinguish," or "apprehend."[2] The Dogon priests say that the mere act of perception causes the perfect order of the primordial waves to be disrupted and creates a kind of chaos that must then be fundamentally reordered and restructured. The stages of this reordering of matter create the po pilu.

In *Point of Origin,* we were able to correlate aspects of various ancient creation traditions and demonstrate how they relate to a single archaic set of concepts. From that perspective, the eight incarnations of the dancing elephant Ganesha in India were shown to reflect symbolism that is a match for the eight progressive stages of the po pilu, as defined in Dogon cosmology. From one perspective in India, Ganesha is the son of the goddess Sati. He was created from clay as a kind of toy doll, granted consciousness so that he could become a real boy, mistakenly beheaded by the god Siva, and then granted a new head, that of a white elephant. In the Tamil language of India, the word *pilu* means "elephant" and "son." For the Dogon, it means "white." In the Turkish language, the word for "elephant" is rendered as *fil*. By comparison, the Icelandic word for "elephant" is *fil*, while in the Faroese language, the word for "elephant" is *filur*. The Faroese word *fil* means "rank, order, or series," terms that are appropriate to Ganesha, who through his eight incarnations symbolizes this reordering of matter. From this same perspective of the story of Ganesha and the reordering of matter, the Faroese word *filt* means "perceived," "sensed," and "conscious."[3]

For reasons that are cosmological in nature, Ganesha is sometimes pictured as having only one spear-like tusk. In some traditions, the arrow is considered to be an icon of Ganesha, or sometimes of his goddess mother. In some languages, the term for "arrow" or "tusk" is rendered as *pille,* a phoneme that, in the mind-set of our cosmology, implies "elephant." So it makes sense that the Faroese word *pilur* means "arrow, dart, barb, spear, javelin."[4]

From one perspective in Dogon cosmology, the processes of creation are categorized into four conceptual stages that would be applicable to any creative act. The Dogon priests illustrate the relationship of these four stages through the example of planning and building a house. In the first stage, referred to as *bummo,* an initial concept for building the structure in a specific place is arrived at. In Egypt, the term is *bu maa,* words that we interpret to mean "place perceived." The likely Faroese correlate to this term is *buo,* which simply means "place."[5] The term for the second Dogon phase is *yala,* which pertains to the idea of initiating the construction project by defining it in broad strokes. In Egypt, the correlate is pronounced *ahau,* meaning "boundaries." A likely Faroese counterpart to these terms is the word *aoal,* meaning "main," "primary," or "fundamental." The Dogon term for the third phase is given as *tonu,* and it represents a stage in which an outline for the structure is roughly marked. The Egyptian term is *tennu,* meaning "estimate." The comparable Faroese word is *toni*, which means "mark" or "engrave." In the last of the four phases, the project is brought to completion. The Dogon term for this stage is *toymu*, meaning "complete." As the Dogon conceptualize it, at completion the project is considered to be "drawn." The Egyptian term is *temau*, which also means "complete." The correlated Faroese term is the word *tøma* (roughly pronounced *tema*), which means "draw" or "delineate."

Initiates to the Dogon creation tradition are given these definitions as a kind of staged metaphor to help them distinguish four categories of symbolic references and place them in the proper relationship to one another. So as the Dogon priests discuss a symbolic term or concept, if they specify that this symbol or word represents the tonu of a concept, the initiate understands this to mean that, symbolically, the term falls within the third of four progressive stages of the concept.

One ancient ritual that we can consider to be a signature of the cosmology we have been pursuing is the practice of circumcision. Herodotus, the early Greek historian of ancient Egypt, was of the opinion that circumcision originated with the ancient Egyptians and was transmitted to other cultures through contact with them. From a cosmological perspective, circumcision re-creates the Dogon figure of the egg in a ball. This is the form of a circle that surrounds a central point—essentially the shape of the Egyptian sun glyph. Scientifically, this same figure appears as the first defined shape of creation. For example, after the big bang, matter is understood to have spaced itself at certain defined intervals, creating this shape. As matter forms, the same shape represents the ways in which gravity distributes itself in relation to mass. From the perspective of biological reproduction, the shape is the image of a DNA molecule viewed from the top.

The concepts of the egg in the ball and the egg of the world reflect symbolism that arguably relates to a *sukkah* in Judaism, a hut that is built from twigs and branches during the eight-day celebration of Sukkhot. (The cosmological symbolism of the Jewish high holy days is defined in the Kabbalist tradition.) The comparable Egyptian term was *skhet,* which Budge defines to mean "a shelter made with leaves and branches."[6] The term is based on the phonetic root *skher,* meaning "to cut, to pierce." So it is significant, first, that there is a Faroese word for "circumcision," which suggests that circumcision (a marker of our cosmological tradition) was practiced in Northern Scotland, and, second, that the word is given as *umskera.*[7] The Faroese term *um* can mean "encircling" or "around."

In Dogon society, the term *faro* is a title that is given to a tribal chief. The word is a likely correlate to the term *pharaoh* in ancient Egypt, which described someone whose role was conceived as the center of Egyptian society. However, there is a neighboring tribe to the Dogon called the Bambara who share much of the Dogon cosmology, including their concept of the po pilu as the egg of the world. For the Bambara, the term *faro* refers to the hub of the starlike rays of the po pilu, or its center point when that structure is conceptualized as a spiral. Given the other cosmological terms that appear to be commonly shared by the Dogon and Faroese languages, it would be hard to believe that the name for the Faroe Islands, which lie in such close proximity with the Orkney Islands, would not have cosmological implications.

Every sixty years, the Dogon observe a grand celebration of the stars of Sirius called the Sigi Festival. The Dogon word *sigi* is a likely correlate to the Egyptian word *skhai,* meaning "to celebrate a festival." At the time of this festival, inner secrets of the Dogon tradition are revealed by the Dogon priests to younger initiates of the tradition. In the Faroese language, the word *siga* means "say, relate, convey, explain, communicate, instruct." These meanings would appear to be given from the perspective of a priest who imparts knowledge. The Faroese word *siggia* means "see, discover, consider, discern, distinguish, know, apprehend," meanings that seem to be given from the perspective of an initiate to a tradition.[8]

The Egyptian word *sa* is one that is associated with the god Osiris and the constellation of Orion. For the Dogon, Orion was one of four constellations whose risings and settings regulated the planting, growing, and harvesting stages of the agricultural cycle. The Faroese word *saa* means "to sow" or "to scatter seed."[9] In the context of so many other matching words, it is reasonable to think that more distant word resemblances such as this one may not be coincidental.

The many parallels we are able to demonstrate between Faroese words and cosmological words of the Dogon and Egyptians are in keeping with the parallels we have cited between other aspects of Skara Brae and the Orkney Island region. They suggest that the Faroese language was associated with a creation tradition that was fundamentally similar to the system of cosmology we have been pursuing in our studies. They imply in yet another way that the people who founded Skara Brae may have been closely connected to the ancient Egyptians of 3200 BCE.

6
COSMOLOGICAL SITES OF THE ORKNEY REGION

There are a number of megalithic sites on Orkney Island, dated to the Neolithic era, that may have cosmological significance and bearing on the village at Skara Brae. During the Neolithic era, a "low road" connected these sites with Skara Brae. In the mythic parlance of ancient Scotland, a "high road" was seen as a "road of the living," and a "low road" as the "road of the dead," and so the designation of "low road" implied an association with an underworld. Based both on the need for a road and the destinations linked by that road, we can infer that the sites were originally seen to be conceptually related to one another.

The first megalithic site on Orkney Island that would merit our attention is called the Watchstone of Stenness, and it consists of a large standing stone set at the point where the Stenness and Harray Lochs meet. The stone marks the way to a nearby Neolithic circle of stones called the Standing Stones of Stenness. Some researchers surmise that the watchstone might have originally been one of a pair of standing stones that, taken together, pointed the way to the stone circle.

For those who are not already aware, the Scottish term *ness* refers to a headland, a point, or a promontory. It is thought to derive from an Old English root *nasse*, which meant "nose."[1] In the Egyptian hieroglyphic language, the word *nes* meant "tongue" and was applied to the name of a plant that was called "tongue of the sea."[2] If we allow for possible Egyptian influences on Orkney Island, then this particular usage suggests that the Scottish word *ness* may also have originally referred to the tongue-shaped bodies of water that often surround a headland, point, or promontory, rather than the stretch of land that extends into the water. Taken with either sense of meaning—headland or tongue-shaped body of water—it seems that the word could have been used to accurately identify the same locales.

Symbolically, the Egyptian word *nes* is written with a glyph whose shape is similar to the blade of a sickle or a scythe ⌐⊤. In Dogon cosmology, this shape (which is alternately conceived of as an adze) is considered to be representative of the earliest stages in the formation of matter. Budge relates the concept of an adze to the word *nu,* which is written with the adze glyph ⌐⟍. In Egypt, the term *nu* constitutes a word for "water," refers to a lake or similar body of water specifically associated with a sacred site or temple, and was the name of a water-related deity. For the Egyptians, *nu* also symbolized the concept of the *primeval waters* from which everything was created. The implication for Stenness is that a piece of land set alongside a body of water that outwardly resembled the shape of an adze might possibly have been selected as a location for the standing stone. In support of this viewpoint, the Egyptian word *nui* means "to watch."[3] The Faroese word for "nose," *nøs,* which we take as a potential alternate root for *ness,* is actually pronounced *nus.*[4]

In the Dogon and Buddhist system of cosmology, the processes of the creation of matter begin with an act of perception that causes matter in its primordial wavelike state to ultimately behave like a particle. This act is sometimes symbolized in the cosmology by the term *watcher.*

The processes that catalyze the formation of matter are explained to Dogon initiates in relation to a specific method for the alignment of a ritual shrine called a granary, which we deem to be a form of stupa. That method starts with a single point or gnomon (perhaps a correlate to this watchstone) that was used to define the center of a circle.

Mathematically, a point represents the simplest of geometric concepts. If, as is sometimes surmised, there had actually been a second watchstone at Stenness, the two stones together, taken as two geometric points, would have defined a line, which is the next most simple geometric construct that relates to a stupa.

The existence of any geometric line brings with it the inherent concept of measuring. The Egyptian term *har*, which matches the phonetic root of the Scottish name Harray, represents the concept of a "measure."[5] For the Dogon and the Buddhists, these three concepts of a point, a line, and a unit of measure can be seen as prerequisites for explaining how matter is created. In ancient times, the unit of measure that was introduced in the cosmology for use by initiates was the cubit, defined as the distance from a person's elbow to the tip of the middle finger, or alternately as the average pace or step of a person. It is of interest that the stretch of land that rests between the Stenness and Harray Lochs actually resembles the forearm shape that defines a cubit, with a finger pointing to the Standing Stones of Stenness.

For the purposes of our studies, we consider the cubit, which is the unit of measure used to align a stupa, to be another signature element of the Dogon and Buddhist system of cosmology. For us, its mere presence among the symbolic concepts of a culture implies the influence of this same cosmology. One good indication that the cubit in Neolithic Orkney was used for this same purpose of alignment is that the Faroese word for "cubit" is actually pronounced *alin*. Likewise, the Faroese word for "watcher" is *siggja*, which reflects the previously discussed Dogon cosmological concept of sigi (the Egyptian skhai), along with its implications of instructed esoteric knowledge.[6]

Within the mind-set of the cosmology and based on these multilingual word meanings and symbolic relationships, it seems quite tenable that the Watchstone of Stenness was meant to represent the first step or stage in the creation of matter—the first ascending step up the conceptual stairway of matter. Appropriate to that interpretation, the Faroese word for "stair" is given as *stupo*.[7]

Located near the Watchstone of Stenness are the Standing Stones of Stenness, which were set in place in Neolithic times on the mainland of Orkney Island, five miles northeast of Stromness. Stenness is considered by many historians to be the oldest henge site in the British Isles. (A henge is a prehistoric monument that consists of a circle of stones or of wooden uprights.)

The Stenness site now holds only three large standing stones. These are seen as the surviving remnants of what is thought to have been an unfinished calendar circle whose plan called for twelve standing stones of comparable size. In 1808, George Barry described Stenness as consisting of both a circle of stones and a semicircle, with some stones "standing irregularly."[8] In the center of the circle sat a dolmen (a simple megalithic tomb) that was composed of three smaller standing stones topped by a flat horizontal stone. One prevailing academic viewpoint is that this central dolmen was a nineteenth-century fabrication, and so not an authentic or original part of the archaic site.[9]

During excavations in the early 1970s, the existence was discovered of a massive square hearth at the center of the Stenness stone circle.

The Standing Stones of Stenness on Orkney Island,
considered to be the oldest henge site in the British Isles.
Used by permission of Orkney Archive and Library.

Suggestions are that an original, smaller square space was enlarged over time, which eventually resulted in this massive hearth. Architectural parallels to a Neolithic house called Barnhouse at a nearby locale suggest that a large house of similar plan once stood at the center of the Stenness circle.[10]

Although it appears that the Stenness stone circle was conceived as a lasting monument, there is also evidence of piecemeal construction over a period of time. For instance, researchers believe that a circular ditch that surrounds the site was a later addition. It is also clear that some planned stones were never actually placed. This implies that the circle was never, in fact, completed.

The concept of standing stones placed in a circle is one that dates from the earliest archaic era of the traditions we study. It was symbolic of an earth mother goddess who was cosmologically linked to the stars of Sirius and whose memory seems to have carried forward in the ancient traditions of Africa, Egypt, India, Tibet, China, Polynesia, and apparently Europe. Typically, a smaller stupa-like shrine, comparable to the disputed Stenness dolmen, was found at the center of the circle. In perhaps its earliest form, this central shrine took the form of a stone cairn built from three stones topped by a flat, horizontal stone, the same configuration as the Stenness dolmen. The French anthropologist Marcel Griaule, who conducted the decades-long study of the Dogon, includes a photograph of a three-stone Dogon cairn in one of his works.

As the Buddhists and Dogon understand and describe this archaic tradition, the stupa constituted the grand mnemonic symbol of an instructed civilizing plan that was founded on (and closely interlinked with) concepts of creation. From the standpoint of an initiate in this tradition, the first civilizing skill to be learned was the method of aligning a stupa-like shrine. This involved the creation of a sacred space, defined as a circle with an inscribed axis whose four radiating arms were aligned to the cardinal points. The alignment was accomplished with a central stick or stone whose shadows were marked like the hours of a sundial at the points where they crossed the circle.

Once completed, this type of circle functioned as a working sundial and so served as a timepiece by which to measure and track the hours of a day. However, the two longest shadows of the day (morning and evening), marked at the points where they intersected the circle, defined the endpoints of an east–west aligned line whose movements during the year could also be used to mark the annual equinoxes and the solstices. This feature of the alignment allowed an initiate to predict the seasons of the year. In other words, once completed, the aligned circle would have acted as both a clock and a calendar.

In our view, this calendrical function, related to marking the agricultural year, was one presumed purpose of the Standing Stones of Stenness. In support of that outlook, Budge lists the Egyptian word *s-ten,* which means "to mark out, to distinguish" and "to distinguish between winter and summer."[11]

We have mentioned that, from a cosmological perspective, this centered circle represents the first defined shape that appears during the process of creation of the universe, of matter, and in biological reproduction. So from a scientific perspective, it seems quite sensible that one of the earliest cosmological structures set in place on Orkney Island seems to have symbolically represented one of the earliest defined stages in cosmological creation.

To the west and slightly north of (and in clear view of) Stenness is the chambered cairn of Maes Howe, a structure that was built nearly four hundred years after the stone circle at Stenness, at around 2800 BCE. Two of the Stenness stones actually frame a view of Maes Howe from where the circle is situated (see top image, next page).

In the illustration on the next page (bottom), we can see that the layout of the Maes Howe site takes the same general form of a stoneless ring or circle defined by a ditch and includes a central hill or mound in place of the stone cairn that stood at the center of the stone circle at Stenness.

From a cosmological perspective, in the appropriate next stage in the creation of matter, mass is described as rising up like a tent cloth

Maes Howe, as visible between two of the Stenness standing stones.
Picture by Keith and Thomas Sisman.

Maes Howe prior to dome reconstruction. Painting by James Farrer.

that has been pulled upward from its center. In some contexts, this is referred to as the primeval mound. Conceptually, this is the stage at which the earliest stirrings of mass are brought forth, to eventually be transformed into fundamental particles. Appropriately, the Egyptian phoneme *mes* (comparable to the Scottish word *meas*) implies the notion of something that is brought forth, born, or produced.[12] The Dogon root *me* refers to a placenta, a biological structure that facilitates biological birth. Genevieve Calame-Griaule writes in the *Dictionnaire Dogon* that the growth of the placenta is compared to the raising upward of "earth" or mass as matter forms.[13]

The Scottish word *howe* comes from the Middle English root *hol,* meaning "hollow."[14] The likely Egyptian correlate to the Scottish term *howe* is pronounced *hau,* which means "hall" or "temple."[15] Looked at in this way, the combined term Meas Howe would imply the notion of a hall or temple dedicated to the raising up of matter. As such, conceptually, physically, and positionally, it would seem to codify a stage of creation that immediately follows what is symbolized at Stenness and so continues a progression of symbolic stages that began with the Watchstone of Stenness.

In its original configuration, the central mound at Meas Howe approximated the shape of a dome—the same essential concept that defines a temple in the archaic tradition of our cosmology. In 1910, when the Maes Howe site came under the care of the state, a concrete roof was added to it, and the mound was reconfigured into a more rounded, dome-like shape. Internally, the structure of the cairn surrounds four chambers, a number that also carries cosmological symbolism. From both an ancient cosmological perspective and a modern scientific one, matter as we know it exists in four dimensions, and in the Dogon tradition these dimensions are characterized as divisions or chambers.

In the Dogon and Buddhist system of cosmology, the first three stages of creation, which we proposed are symbolized by the Neolithic structures on Orkney Island, lead to the formation of the Dogon egg of the world. This "egg" is defined as a kind of bundle of eight wrapped-up dimensions, comparable to a Calabi-Yau space in string theory, which is the currently favored scientific theory for how matter forms. The Neolithic low road from Maes Howe led ultimately to Skara Brae, which was a village that consisted of a bundled group of eight houses. We have mentioned that one Egyptian term that relates to the Dogon "egg" is *skhet*. Appropriately, an Egyptian term that is based on the same phonetic root, pronounced *skheru,* means "chambers."[16]

The clear suggestion is that the Neolithic stone structures on Orkney Island, although implemented over a period of time that spanned several centuries, must have been initially conceived of as a group and intended to represent progressive stages of creation. It's also clear that those stages of creation were defined in the same essential symbolic, linguistic, and scientific terms as the Dogon and Buddhist system of cosmology. From that perspective, the suggestion is that the village of Skara Brae should be seen as much more than just a peaceful Neolithic farming village. Clearly the structures of the village played an important role in the symbolic progression that was introduced by the other sites.

In addition to these early megalithic sites that were linked by a Neolithic low road, also we know of later sites on Orkney Island. About five miles northeast of Stenness stands a second ring of stones comparable to but smaller than the Standing Stones of Stenness. It is referred to as the Ring of Brodgar (or Brogar). This ring has never been fully excavated, so its precise age has not been definitively established. The presumption is that it was constructed between 2500 BCE and 2000 BCE, and so it would have been the last of the known stone structures to be built on Orkney Island that might relate to Neolithic times.

Both the Egyptian and Faroese phonemes *bro* imply the concept of duality or of a brother or sibling. The Dogon phoneme *bor* implies the concept of giving birth; it is defined as the idea of pushing one object through a smaller opening. Appropriately, that meaning would place the cosmological symbolism of Brodgar at the final stage of creation. The phonetic value *ga* is an archaic one, and for the Dogon and Egyptians it implies the notion of a division or stage of creation. In the Faroese language, the phoneme *gar* associates with concepts that define enclosures, such as an embankment, a court, a courtyard, or a hall.

Between Stenness and the Ring of Brodgar lies the Ness of Brodgar, which is described as a "temple complex" and may include up to one hundred buildings. Although the site is not thought to have been inhabited all year round, in the era just following Skara Brae's habitation it is thought to have become the epicenter of ritual activity in the region. By 2012, only about 10 percent of this site had been excavated, but expectations were that it would eventually shed new light on how people on Orkney Island lived during Neolithic times.[17]

7
THE DOGON FIELD OF AROU

In Dogon cosmology, the egg of the world, which we proposed was represented by the village of Skara Brae, is the first finished structure of matter. Like the Calabi-Yau space, this structure is envisioned to exist at every point in space-time and is the foundation on which larger components of matter, such as the atom, are built. Therefore, when we talk about the ascending stages of matter, it is clear that the egg of the world does not constitute the uppermost step of the staircase. So the question arises as to whether an attempt was made on Orkney Island to represent any additional stages of matter that would have followed Skara Brae as the Dogon egg of the world. According to the Dogon priests, the eighth vibration of matter pierces the egg and initiates the formation of a new egg. These eggs in series, which are compared in the Buddhist tradition to pearls on a string, then form membranes. The ascending processes eventually lead us to 266 fundamental "seeds" or "signs" of matter, which we take as likely counterparts to the more than two hundred distinct particles of matter that have been documented to exist through modern particle bombardment.

From the perspective of string theory, particles of matter as we perceive them are actually the product of the vibrations of microscopic threads. Each frequency of vibration, like different notes played on a stringed instrument, corresponds to a type of fundamental particle as we conceptualize it. This outlook agrees with the view of the Dogon priests, who describe matter as being "woven" from vibrating threads.

From a scientific perspective, the concept of a vibration is given in terms of the frequency with which the vibration repeats, which is sometimes depicted graphically by a wavy line that moves repeatedly up and down ᰠᰠᰠ. The vibrations of matter are understood to take place within the context of what is called the *background field*. The correlate to these vibrations on a macrocosmic level now consists of a kind of radiational glow that is thought to be a leftover remnant of the big bang explosion that created the universe.

Every year, just before the sowing of the seeds for a new agricultural season, the Dogon create a field drawing that is meant to symbolize these fundamental vibrations of matter, set against the backdrop of a primal field, symbolized by an actual agricultural field. The figure consists of a circle that is drawn in the soil with a stick and is then filled in with a series of zigzagging lines to symbolize all of the diverse vibrations of matter (see image on next page).

For the Dogon, the "seeds" of matter that these zigzag lines represent are the domain of a priest called the Hogon of Arou. The Dogon term *hogon* refers to an initiated priestly elder (reminiscent of the Cohane in Judaism) who is revered for his wisdom and knowledge of cosmology. The comparable Faroese word *hogur* means "eminent," "distinguished," or "dignified."[1] The Dogon figure is also drawn on a platform as part of the ceremony that is observed whenever a new priest is ordained as the new Hogon of Arou.[2] According to Marcel Griaule, in the past the whole set of signs was carved on the entry door of the Arou priest. Looked at in this way, the field in which the figure is drawn can be referred to as the Field of Arou.

Arou was the name of the founding ancestor of Dogon culture. It is the name of the largest of four ancestral family lineages of the Dogon tribe,[3] and the Hogon of Arou is considered to be the most important leader in the tribe. The word *arou* also is the name given to a white tunic that is considered to be traditional clothing of the Dogon tribe. By comparison to the Dogon term *arou,* which we have said is assigned

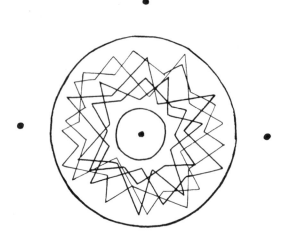

Dogon field drawing
from The Pale Fox *by Marcel Griaule*
and Germaine Dieterlen.

to an annual ritual that relates to the concept of primordial vibrations, in Faroese, the word *ar* means "year," *arla* means "primordial" or "primeval," and *aralag* means "pulsation," a concept that implies the notion of vibration.[4]

Egyptian words that are formed on the phonetic value *ar* carry meanings that clearly pertain to our discussion of cosmology and to this Dogon agricultural ritual. The first is a word, *ar*, that means "to create" and so would refer to the overall process we have been exploring.[5] The related term *arit* is defined as the seven divisions of the Tuat, which is the term for the Egyptian Underworld, which we associate with these stages of matter. We consider the Egyptian Tuat to be a correlate of the Dogon Second World of matter.[6] In our view, the divisions of the Tuat are counterparts to the divisions of the egg of the world.

Also appropriate to these stages of creation, Budge defines the Egyptian term *aaru* to mean "transformations." This term describes the changes in state through which these primordial particles are said to have passed.[7] The Egyptian word *aarat* means "to plant," so it conveys the same sense of meaning as "sowing seeds," the event that coincides with the timing of the Dogon agricultural field ritual.[8] Lastly, the Egyptian word *ar* also means "door," the locale, related to the Dogon Hogon of Arou, on which Griaule said the figures were inscribed. Each of the eight stages of the egg of the world is associated with a door or gateway to the next stage.

Because the Skara Brae field holds the same place as the Field of Arou in what can be taken as a specific cosmological progression, the clear suggestion is that on Orkney Island, as in Dogon culture, the fields that were sown by the farmers of the village of Skara Brae also carried cosmological symbolism. If so, their placement in series with structures that represent other ascending steps of creation served to define the next progressive stage of matter: the sowing of the primordial seeds of matter. As such, we could say that, cosmologically speaking, the farmers' field takes us one conceptual step further beyond the eight-chambered houses of Skara Brae.

8

THE FIELD OF AROU AND THE ELYSIAN FIELDS

Given the significance in Dogon cosmology of the concept of the Field of Arou and its apparent parallels at Skara Brae, it makes sense to ask whether the ancient Egyptians might have also preserved a similar concept. In truth, since we believe the Dogon to have essentially been Egyptian at 3200 BCE (the era when Skara Brae is thought to have been founded), then from the perspective we are entertaining, it would have been Egyptians, not yet the Dogon, who actually carried the tradition to Skara Brae.

One Egyptian word for "field or meadow" is *sekh-t*.[1] Symbolically, it reads "cultivated field" 𓇏 "of matter" ⌒, followed by a straight vertical line that we take to indicate the definition of a concept |. The glyph that conveys the meaning of "cultivated field" is the image of three reedleaf glyphs, separated by what might represent three planted seeds.

Using the Egyptian word *sekh-t* as the basis for a search of Budge's dictionary, we soon locate a term that is an apparent match for our Dogon Field of Arou. Budge gives it as Sekh-t Aaru.[2] He lists the term in a section of his dictionary that consists largely of names of geographical places. Similarly, we find that the Egyptian word *aaru* means "reeds,"[3] so Budge defines the term Sekh-t Aaru, which is a simple compound of those two terms combined, to mean "Field of Reeds." However, he states that this term is also a name for a geographical locale we have always believed to be quasi-mythical, called the Elysian Fields.

In Greek mythology, the Elysian Fields (also called Elysium) were an archaic counterpart to the modern concept of heaven. This was the place where heroes who had gained the favor of the gods were ostensibly sent to be buried. The Elysian Fields were sometimes characterized as the Isles of the Blessed or the Fortunate Isles, representing the very vision of an ideal afterlife. Homer describes the Elysian plain as a land of perfect happiness.[4] In Greek, the term Blessed Isles is given as Nesoi Makaron. In chapter 6, we focused on the Egyptian word *nes* during our discussion of the location of the Watchstone of Stenness. The word referred to tongue-shaped bodies of water, such as those found on Orkney Island. In Egyptian, the word *maa* means "boat," *mai* means "island," and *maak* means "protector."[5] From that perspective, the term Nesoi Makaron could refer to the Islands of the Nesses or Islands of the Protectors.

Homer also wrote in the *Odyssey* that the Elysian Fields lay on the western margin of the Earth, surrounded by the encircling stream of Oceanus. Hesiod makes reference to the "Isles of the Blessed," located in the Western Ocean. Some ancient sources asserted that mortals had, in fact, visited the Elysian Fields without actually having suffered death in order to experience for themselves what a future heaven would be like. The Theban poet Pindar described the Elysian Fields as a single island, which he called the White Isle, a place to which Achilles was said to have been transported.

We know from the absence of weaponry among the excavated artifacts at Skara Brae that it was a peaceful place and obviously not one prone to local disputes. One Faroese term for both "blessed" and "lucky/fortunate" is *saela*. We see this as a compound word and interpret it to mean "to sow happiness."[6] From this perspective, the *el* in the term Elysian would refer to the concept of happiness.

Among these various descriptions, we find statements that seem to align well with the attributes of Orkney Island. As Pindar asserted, the White Isle is an island surrounded by ocean and is located to the west of Greece, at the edge of the Atlantic, which fits Orkney Island. Additionally, Orkney Island is known for its stunning white beaches and so could reasonably be characterized as the White Isle. The question of whether Maes Howe ever served as an actual tomb for bodies is still academically debated, since all that survives now, after a period of five thousand years, are trace remains. But some researchers interpret the structure as having been a burial site for certain elite members of the Neolithic society. Whether those burials might have been granted as a reward for honored heroes is uncertain. One indication that they might have been is found in the Faroese term for "hero," which is *hetja*.[7] The term *het* is an Egyptian word for "temple" or "hall," a homonym for the word that means "heart." (One defining attribute of terms of the ancient cosmology is that they carry multiple discrete meanings.) Similarly, the Faroese term for "reward" is *samsyna,* outwardly similar to the name of the biblical hero Samson.

Donald Redford characterizes the Egyptian Field of Reeds or Field of Rushes as a counterpart to the Greek Elysian Fields; however, he places its locale (based on Egyptian sources) in the East. He tags the location to the place where the sun renews itself after setting. He describes it as being "really an inundated marshland divided by lakes and canals; according to the Pyramid Texts, the sun god purifies himself in the morning in the Lake of the Field of Rushes . . . the deceased, often accompanied by his wife, is shown paddling across the waterways of these fields in his boat and plowing, sowing, reaping and threshing, often dressed in beautiful white linen garments."[8] In contrast to that, Egyptian tomb inscriptions that discuss the afterlife describe the deceased as wanting "to walk on the beautiful ways of the west."[9]

Henri Frankfort writes in *Ancient Egyptian Religion* that the Egyptian belief was that a dead person must cross water in order to reach the Elysian Fields. Once across, that journey took the person along a road past a series of obstacles that led ultimately to the field. The notion of the placement and removal of obstacles is one that defines Ganesha's role in our archaic cosmology. We argue in *Point of Origin* that the eight incarnations of Ganesha represent the eight staged gateways of the egg of the world—the same stages of creation that we propose are represented by the megalithic sites on Orkney Island. The *sieve,* which also symbolizes those gateways, is a term that is offered as a kind of metaphor for an obstacle that can be either destructive or productive, in that it serves to separate solid (material) things from less solid (nonmaterial) ones. For example, the Dogon use a sieve to separate beans from the sand in which the beans are preserved.[10]

Frankfort quotes a Pyramid Text in which Pharaoh Pepi comes to purify himself at the Field of Reeds. (Note that the Egyptian name Pepi bears a phonetic resemblance to the name of the Papae clerics who were described as originally inhabiting Orkney Island.) Pepi descends from there (in our earthly conception, returns back along the Neolithic low road) to the Sekhet Hetep, or Field of Offerings, meaning the megalithic Orkney Island sites. The Egyptian term Sekhet Hetep is written using the same three reedleaf glyphs that define the term Sekhet Aaru. Frankfort, apparently not cognizant of the dualistic view as held by the Dogon in which the Field of Arou represents both cosmological concept and the actual physical locale of an agricultural field, writes that "this name (Field of Offerings) seems odd for a place of lasting life."[11]

Other descriptive details about the Field of Reeds are included in *The Egyptian Book of the Dead,* alternately referred to as the *Book of Coming Forth by Day.* Chapter 6 of the book tells of the types of agricultural work that the deceased could be required to do in the Field of Reeds. Images in Egyptian art depict the dead happily performing these tasks. Such references show that, like the Dogon field and the Skara Brae site on Orkney Island, the Egyptian Field of Reeds was understood to represent an idyllic, productive farming community.

Chapter 110 of the *The Egyptian Book of the Dead* states, "Here begin the spells for the Fields of Offerings, the spells for coming forth by day, to enter and leave the world of the dead, to travel to the Fields of Reeds, to meet in the Fields of Offerings, the great place of winds, and there to be powerful, blessed, to work, to harvest, to eat, to drink, to make love, to do everything one does on earth."[12] This Egyptian reference to the Field of Reeds as a "place of winds" agrees with a 1908 passage authored by an early Orkney Island researcher named Magnus Spence, who described the island's climate. He wrote, "[Orkney Island's] one outstanding characteristic is wind. No other region in Great Britain can compare with it for the violence and frequency of its winds."[13]

There is another, overtly cosmological reason to associate the term *el* with Orkney Island. During the course of our studies, we have observed a consistent naming convention for ancient cultures that shared the Dogon/Egyptian cosmology. According to this convention, the name of the culture was a compound term that included the name of the deity, or personified stage of creation, that the culture specifically celebrated. It was as if the cultures were college students who chose to declare their major subjects through their names. These names often were expressed using permutations of the Egyptian term *skhai*, meaning "to celebrate." From this perspective, the predynastic Amazigh (Amma Skhai) tribes in Egypt, like the Dogon, celebrated the creator god Amma. The Na-Khi, or Na-Xi, of Tibet celebrated the Neith-like mother goddess Na. The Chinese creator god Pau-Xi's name reflected celebration of the po or pau, which is the name for the Dogon correlate to an atom.

At Orkney Island, we find the village of Skara Brae situated on the Bay of Skaill. From the perspective of our cosmological naming convention, we could interpret that to have been Skhai El, "celebrates *el*." Looked at from the viewpoint that the word *el* refers to happiness, the term could mean "celebrates happiness," a definition that suits the quasi-mythical Elysian Fields. Likewise, the god El is considered by some researchers to be a surrogate of the Hebrew god Yahweh. In support of that view, we consider the two Hebrew *yud* characters that serve as placeholders for the name of God in Hebrew texts to be counterparts to two Egyptian reedleaf glyphs ⎞⎞. These reedleaf glyphs, in turn, might well be symbolic of Orkney Island and the concept of the Elysian Fields or Field of Reeds. Meanwhile, the name Yahweh is understood to have been an anagram that combines four Hebrew letters, *yud, hay, vav,* and *hay,* which can again serve as placeholders for the name of the Hebrew god. However, these letters symbolize the temporal concepts of "was, is, and will be," which constitute a signature phrase of the Egyptian mother goddess Neith (or Net) and are inscribed on her temple as "I am all that was, is, or will be."

Based on the presumption that Orkney Island was the locale described as the Elysian Fields, the color white—which the ancient Greek philosophers identify with the fields—is one that is expressly associated in the archaic mother goddess tradition with nonmaterial spirituality. White is also a color that, from a cosmological standpoint, implies the notion of light. We can infer that the Hebrew god Yahweh was seemingly cast as a Light God (since his first official act in the biblical book of Genesis was to create light). In support of this view is a Faroese term *al* (based on a modified *a* sound that causes it to be pronounced as *el*). It means "ray," in the sense of a "beam of light."[14]

Light is also the essential nature of the spiritual principle that ostensibly intertwines with a material principle to create our physical universe. This entwined aspect of the cosmology seems to be reflected at Skara Brae, where eight stone chambers may have been interspersed with white sand to create the contours of the village. All of these associations strengthen potential correlations between a god named El, who we think may have been celebrated on Orkney Island, and the Hebrew god Yahweh. Knowing all of that, it seems interesting that the Icelandic term for "island" is given as *eyjan.* This word is a correlate to the Faroese term *oyggj,* which also means "island."[15] In the Scottish-Gaelic language, the word for "island" is *eilean.* From that perspective, it could make sense that the fields on the island of the god El might come to be known as the *El eyjan* fields.

9

FURTHER CORRELATIONS TO FAROESE WORDS

Throughout this volume we have made reference to words of the Faroese language whose pronunciations and meanings compare favorably with those of the Dogon and Egyptian hieroglyphic languages. These are words that have bearing on concepts of cosmology we have discussed. However, when we simply browse through a Faroese-English dictionary, we encounter a number of additional words whose phonetic roots and meanings also seem familiar to us from our studies in ancient cosmology. Most linguists will say that simple word-to-word comparisons between two languages, outside of the context of other confirming evidence, are not sufficient to demonstrate an etymological link between the words. This is because most languages define only around forty phonetic values—too few to rule out simple coincidence as the likely cause of any outward similarity between two words. Nonetheless, given the complex interrelationship of cosmological terms we have seen so far in this study, it makes sense that we at least mention other Faroese words whose pronunciations and meanings could suggest the influence of this same system of cosmology.

Although we have discussed some aspects of the word previously, perhaps the first of these words would be the term *faro*, which for the Dogon is a title of ancestral chieftainship. The word is also phonetically similar to the Egyptian word *pharaoh*, a person who bore responsibility for maintaining order and stability in ancient Egyptian society. One comparable Faroese word is *faoir,* meaning "father."[1] The word *faro* plays an obvious role in the Skara Brae region as the name of a group of islands just north of Orkney Island, known as the Faroes. Suggestively, the Faroe Islands are home to their own set of pyramid-shaped structures, including a mountain called Kirvi, whose name is similar to the Faroese term *kervi,* meaning "system."[2]

In the archaic tradition that we trace to locales like Gobekli Tepe in Turkey, birds of prey like the vulture and the falcon became symbols of deity. In later historical times they came to be symbols of the pharaohs in Egypt, who were seen as representatives of deity. So it is interesting that the Faroese word for "falcon" is given as *faroafalkur,* which is also founded on the phonetic root *faro.*[3] The same archaic deities, whose icons include birds of prey, are remembered fondly in many of the cultures we study as knowledgeable instructors who brought skills of civilization to humanity, such as those of agriculture. The Faroese word *faro* conveys a similar outlook in its definitions "teach," "educate," "train," and "instruct."[4] A breed of falcon called the merlin is the only modern-day bird of prey found on the Faroe Islands. The falcon is a bird that has close association to royalty in ancient Egypt. In the Faroese language, another word for "falcon" is *smyril.*[5] Consonant with that pronunciation, Budge defines the term *smer* to be an Egyptian title of nobility.[6]

Next on our list of comparative words is the name of the Dogon creator god Amma. The Dogon priests consider Amma to be dual in nature, so the deity can be interpreted as being both male and female. The Dogon egg-in-the-ball shape (the circle that encloses a central dot) is alternately referred to as a picture of Amma. The name Amma was Ganesha's affectionate nickname for his mother Sati. For the Dogon, the word *amma* also means "to grasp," "to hold firm," or "to establish." The name is alternately given in some archaic traditions as Uma. At the bottom of the symbolism is the notion of a mother goddess who embraces humanity and of a nonmaterial universe that can be said to entwine with a material one. A comparable Faroese term is pronounced *um* and means "about," in the sense of "encircling" or "encompassing."[7] The Faroese word *umfero* defines the concept of a cycle.[8]

There is a character in Dogon mythology named Ogo who plays the cosmological role of *light*. He is a likely counterpart to an Egyptian Light God named Aakhu. In the story from a Dogon myth, Ogo believes he can create a universe as perfect as Amma's and so breaks off a square piece of Amma's placenta and essentially expands that piece to create our material universe. There is a comparable Faroese term *okja,* which means "to enlarge," "to expand," or "to amplify."[9]

We have mentioned that in the Dogon and Egyptian traditions, the term *nu* referred to the primordial waters, the underlying wave-like source from which everything in our material universe emerges. For both cultures, the concept of nu lies outside the bounds of space and time. Appropriate to that definition, the Faroese term *nu* means "now," in the sense of "immediately" or "instantly."[10] The term *nu* also refers to water, one of the four primordial elements of water, fire, wind, and earth. The primordial element of fire is linked in our cosmology to the concept of perception and the act of seeing. For the Dogon and Egyptians, these concepts relate to the phoneme *ma*. A likely Faroese counterpart to this term is *møta,* which, as we noted in chapter 5, means "to see."[11]

The cosmological phoneme *ta* refers to the concept of earth, which we interpret to symbolize mass. In accord with that meaning, the name of the earth mother goddess in the Sakti tradition is Tana Penu. We see similar implications for the Faroese word *taoa,* which means "to fertilize" or "to cultivate."[12]

10

ARGAT: AN ANCIENT NAME FOR ORKNEY ISLAND

We have devoted some effort and have had a fair amount of success correlating Faroese, Egyptian, and Dogon words of cosmology. These correlations suggest that there were coherent Egyptian-related influences at work in the Orkney Island vicinity at or around 3200 BCE. Knowing this to be likely, it may be instructive to attempt to interpret various ancient place names from the Orkney region in relation to Egyptian and Dogon words to see if we can bring some sense to their meanings.

An obvious place to start this process might be with an ancient name for Orkney Island itself, which was given as Argat. There is an Egyptian word *ar* that means "to ascend," and it is expressed symbolically in relation to images of an ascending staircase.[1] We have mentioned that in Egypt, the term *arit* is assigned to the seven divisions of the Tuat, which, based on Dogon definitions, we correlate to the first seven conceptual steps in the ascension of matter. Budge tells us that "each of the *arits* was in charge of a watcher, a doorkeeper, and a herald."[2]

We recall that during our comparison of Skara Brae and Dogon house plans in chapter 4, we explored the meanings of the Faroese word *gatt,* the Dogon word *ga,* and the Egyptian word *hetgat* and found that they refer to the concepts of a threshold, a doorway, or a gate. In *Point of Origin,* we discussed the term *ga* as it relates both to incarnations of the Vedic elephant god Ganesha and to conceptual stages in the formation of matter. Ganesha's traditional role in the mythology of ancient India was as a gatekeeper for his mother Sati, whom, as noted previously, he affectionately called Amma. We also interpreted Sati's consort Siva to represent the concept of a sieve, a concept that the Dogon apply metaphorically to their egg of the world.

Given all of this, it seems we are on firm ground to interpret the suffix *-gat* of the term Argat to refer to divisions or gateways that would be comparable to those between conceptual stages in the formation of the egg of the world. From that perspective, the term Argat would represent a compound word (similar to other terms of our cosmology) that means "the ascending gateways of matter." This phrase restates precisely what we argue the series of symbolic structures on Orkney Island were meant to physically represent.

If we were to correlate the Orkney Island structures to written Egyptian symbols, the Watchstone of Stenness is a conceptual correlate to a single reedleaf glyph $\big\rvert$. In our view, the reedleaf represents the concept of "that which is" and so defines the first stage of creation as matter emerges. The circular Standing Stones of Stenness create a structural figure that is a correlate to the Egyptian sun glyph $\odot$. It represents the concept of a measurable unit of time and so defines a second stage of matter, that in which the appearance of *mass* enables *time* to exist.

The two stones that frame the view of Maes Howe from Stenness are conceptual correlates to two Egyptian reedleef glyphs $\big\rvert\big\rvert$. In the Egyptian hieroglyphic language we interpret these to read "that which is, is," and so define the concept of *existence.* This is a third stage of creation, which we again see to be a by-product of the existence of mass and time. As we said in chapter 8, we also equate the two reedleaf glyphs to the two Hebrew yud characters that take the place of the name of God in written Hebrew texts. Commensurate with our outlook on this

Hebrew god as having been a Light God, the image we see of Maes Howe between the two reedlike viewing stones at Stenness offers us a practical demonstration of light's existence by framing the image of the next conceptual stage of creation. Again, we understand light to be a by-product of the creation of mass and time.

We interpret the Maes Howe complex itself to represent the concept of mass as it is raised upward. The image it presents is a correlate to the Egyptian hemisphere glyph ⌂, which we understand to symbolize the concept of mass or matter. The symbolic progression from a single reedleaf at Stenness to two reedleafs at the viewing slot for Maes Howe to, finally, a glyph that depicts three reedleafs in the Egyptian term for the Elysian Fields constitutes the conceptual "reeds" that are referred to in the term Field of Reeds. On the other hand, the climate and topography of Orkney Island, which promote the growth of water-based reeds, suggest the possible existence of an actual Field of Reeds located there in ancient times, which could be a possible source of the Egyptian term.

Knowing that each symbol of astrophysical creation also carries a secondary meaning within the cosmology, one that relates to the processes of biological creation, it seems clear that meanings from this second theme would also have been implied by the structures on Orkney Island. From that perspective, the Watchstone represents a mother's fertilized egg—the same essential symbolism as is assigned to the Dogon god Amma, who resides conceptually at the center point of the egg in a ball. The circle of the Standing Stones of Stenness constitutes the full egg-in-a-ball figure and stands for a developing egg. Considered from a biological perspective, the two viewing stones suggest divisions of the egg as it grows. And finally, Maes Howe would present the image of an expanding womb.

From yet another perspective, there also appears to have been symbolism for these structures that relates to societal definitions of time. From this perspective, the concept of simple existence, represented by the Watchstone, expands to represent an actual *moment in a life* at the stone circle of Stenness. At Maes Howe, we find the egg in a ball, which is typically given as a *symbol of birth,* but it is counterintuitively configured here as a tomb and so simultaneously conveys the *concept of death.* Taken together, these two connotations (birth and death) symbolically suggest the span of a single lifetime. The village of Skara Brae presents an example of a small community, which becomes a home to the concurrent lifetimes of more than one individual. The image of three reedleafs alternating with three seeds 𓇊 , which appears in Egyptian names for the Field of Reeds, could imply the notion of succeeding generations of lifetimes.

Additional insight into the meaning of the term Argat and its possible relationship to the concept of the Elysian Fields may be found in the Greek myth of the ship *Argo* and its crew, the Argonauts. In the storyline of the myth, one of the heroes who joined the Argonauts was Orpheus. He had fallen in love with a beautiful woman named Eurydice, who was tragically killed while listening to him play his lyre. Orpheus was devastated by the death of Eurydice and so appealed to a Greek god and was ultimately granted entrance to the Underworld in hopes of bringing her back from the dead. In this journey, Orpheus is described as descending into the Underworld, which implies that his return trip would require him to "ascend," the same term that we associate with the progressive stages of the formation of matter. In the end, Orpheus's effort to rescue Eurydice failed. However, when Orpheus later died, we are told that he returned to the Underworld and found Eurydice there, waiting for him in the Elysian Fields.[3]

In Greek mythology, titles for the realm of the Underworld and the Elysian Fields were often given as descriptive terms, rather than as proper names. One such term was Domos Haidou, or Domain of Hades.[4] Appropriate to that term, in the Faroese language, the bottommost layer of something, like the Underworld in relation to the living world, was defined by the word *haedd.*[5] Some sources see an evolution in the concept of the Elysian Fields in Greek times. One commentator writes, "Homer knows of no such realm, and consigns all of his heroes to the common house of Haides."[6] However, if we assign the physical locale of the Elysian Fields to Orkney Island and the Greek term Domos Haidou to the same root as the Faroese word *haedd*, then it becomes clear that Homer's concept actually aligns with that same physical locale.

Associations between this Dogon Second World of matter and a spiritual underworld like Hades actually serve to affirm the influence of the archaic tradition we assign to the ancient cosmology. In *Point of Origin* we discussed likely correlations between the mother goddess Sati and modern concepts of Satan. These become evident in ancient Egyptian words that are founded on the phonetic root *sat*.

As is related in the myth of Orpheus, to reach the Elysian Fields required a journey along a path or road. Homer writes in the *Odyssey*, "So did these ghosts travel on together squeaking, while easeful Hermes led them down [to the Land of the Dead] through the ways of dankness. They passed the streams of Okeanos, the White Rock (*petra Leuka*), the Gates of the Sun (*pylai Hêlioi*) and the Land of Dreams (*demos oneiroi*), and soon they came to the field of asphodel, where the souls (*psykhai*), the phantoms (*eidola*) of the dead have their habitation."[7]

By our interpretation, the "streams of Okeanos" represent the inlet waters of the Atlantic Ocean that surround Orkney Island. In fact, the Greek term Okeanos might be taken as an overt reference by Homer to Orkney Island. The "White Rock" represents the Watchstone of Stenness, and the "Gates of the Sun" refers to the viewing stones at Stenness. By this scheme, the "Land of Dreams" would seem to be a reference to Skara Brae itself. It is interesting that Homer equates the term "souls" with the word *psykhai*, since the Faroese word for "soul," *sal*, also means "psyche."[8]

Justification for identifying the village of Skara Brae with Homer's "Land of Dreams" is found in relation to ancient Egyptian words. The Egyptian term *skhet* is one that we associate with the Dogon egg of the world and is what we proposed the eight chambers at Skara Brae to symbolize. In fact, the word Skara itself shares a phonetic root with the term *skhet*. We have said that the Egyptian term *skhet* also refers to a "shelter built from leaves and branches," which is a working description of a Jewish sukkah. Budge lists an Egyptian word for "dream" or "remembrance" that is pronounced *sukka*.

In accordance with the Elysian Field's theme of death, the Egyptian word *sukhet* means "to embalm," and the term *suh ikh* refers to a "reunion of spirits."[9] From this perspective, the Greek Underworld takes on the same symbolic associations to the Dogon Second World of matter as we have previously proposed for the Egyptian Underworld.

The stages of creation that play out in the Neolithic structures on Orkney Island re-create the same sequence of shapes that is evoked during the alignment of a Buddhist stupa and in the aligned Dogon granary structure. The Dogon define their structure in relation to the term *ark,* and the symbolism they assign to the term is also reflected in the Buddhist stupa. Those commonalities suggest that similarities between the term *ark* and the archaic name Argat may not be coincidental.

In *Point of Origin,* we discussed several Egyptian words that we interpreted to be names of archaic sanctuaries. These names, which do not seem to follow the same phonetic rules as later historic Egyptian words, do seem to observe certain conventions. Typically they were defined in relation to the term *get* or *het,* which implied the notion of a sanctuary or temple. Likewise, since the earliest such sanctuaries were often situated in high mountain locales, the words ended with the Egyptian three-humped mountain glyph ᴖᴖ. Traditional Egyptologists often take this glyph as a determinative to indicate the name of a place in a foreign country.

Budge defines a term *arq-hehtt* that fits our criteria for the name of one of these archaic sanctuaries but also presents an excellent phonetic and conceptual match for the term Argat.[10] Interpreted simply as a compound word, the term *arq-hehtt* means "temple of the ark," conceived as the stages of creation that are codified in the structure of an aligned

shrine—the same stages that we assign to the Orkney Island megalithic sites, whose structures reflect the same cosmological shapes. From
a Dogon perspective, these stages define processes that occur in the
Second World of matter. Budge defines the term *arq-hehtt* to be a name
for the Other World. The Egyptian term O*ther World* is another
name for the Tuat, which like the Elysian Fields was considered to be a
realm for the deceased. Later religious traditions preserve the word *ark*
as the name of Noah's boat, and the term is not unlike the name of the
mythical Greek boat the *Argo*.

Supportive of this viewpoint, there is an ancient Egyptian text
titled "The Fields of Paradise," which is reproduced in a book edited
by James B. Pritchard called *Ancient Near-Eastern Texts Relating to
the Old Testament*. It is clear from this text that death in the physical world was associated with the region of the sunset (in the west),
while rebirth in the spiritual universe was attained by passing through
the doors of heaven associated with the sunrise (in the east). These
assignments agree with Buddhist concepts of ascension that place a
conceptual gate-of-exit from the material to a nonmaterial universe
at Sirius, a star that is associated symbolically with the east. Based
on these definitions, any physical-world counterpart to this spiritual
field of paradise could reasonably be located in the west, as the Greek
authors assert. A note to the text states, "The Elysian Fields of the
Egyptians included a *sekhet iaru* 'Field of Reeds' and a *sekhet hetep*
'Field of Offerings.'"[11] Our understanding of the term *het,* which is
discussed at length in *Point of Origin,* is that it refers to the concept
of a temple or sanctuary, comparable to the one at Gobekli Tepe that
features circles of standing megalithic stone pillars.

Based on examples given in *Point of Origin,* there are certain features we would expect to see in a truly archaic name for a sanctuary that we do not see in the Egyptian term *arq-hehtt*. In the archaic
forms we have discussed, the term for "temple" is given as *get,* not
as *het*. This difference suggests that the original term may have been
given as a guttural *ch*. In the archaic forms the phoneme *get* appears

as the leading segment of the word, not the trailing segment. In traditional views of the Egyptian hieroglyphic language, the meaning of a word can be refined through the use of *determinatives,* unpronounced glyph shapes that typically fall at the end of the word. As an example, the name of an Egyptian deity may be followed by a glyph that generically pictures a god or a goddess. In archaic word forms, we can find similar determinative glyphs at the front or back end of a word. Likewise, the archaic sanctuary names appear to have been formulated in relation to three astronomic bodies or deities, while this one is defined in relation to the aligned ritual shrine and stages of creation. These kinds of deviation from typical archaic forms make sense for a site such as Skara Brae, which is reasonably thought to have been founded at around 3200 BCE, rather than in the 10,000 BCE era that we associated with the Turkish site of Gobekli Tepe in *Point of Origin.*

Another feature of the archaic sanctuaries that were situated in locales foreign to Egypt is that they were traditionally linked phonetically to the name of a kind of "sister" temple in Egypt, one that was active during historical times. We can see this may also be true of *arq-hehtt.* Budge lists among his names of geographical places a sanctuary called Het-ar[12] at a place identified as Kom, which he surmises to be Ombos, near the modern city of Kawm Umbu. The geographical locale of this site in Egypt is near Aswan. Symbolically, its name reads "temple" ⬚ "of matter's" ⌒ "gateway" ⬚ "which is" ⎛ "the egg's" ◯ "image" ⎛, an interpreted meaning that aptly defines the series of structures we see on Orkney Island. Here the glyph for "temple" takes an archaic form, one that we argue was also found at the exceedingly ancient megalithic site of Gobekli Tepe in Turkey and that we consider to be one starting point for our tradition.

Homer's use of the name Okeanos in connection with the Elysian Fields constitutes a likely reference to Orkney Island and suggests that the *or* in Orkney may also relate to the phonetic value *ar* in Argat. From this perspective, the word Orkney may have combined the term *ar,* meaning "stages of ascension," with the Faroese word *kenna,* meaning "to experience, to grasp, to understand."[13] These terms combined would define Orkney Island as a place where initiates came to experience the constructs of creational cosmology firsthand, on a human scale.

11

ORKNEY ISLAND AS AN ARCHAIC SANCTUARY

Cultural memory of revered ancestor-teachers who are described as the bringers of civilizing knowledge is a common feature of the ancient cultures we study. However, the Dogon provide us with the most specific information about who these teachers may have been and how they approached their apparent task of educating humanity. Both the Dogon and the Buddhists overtly credit this civilizing knowledge to a "nonhuman source." However, the Dogon priests are somewhat more specific than the Buddhists in stating that these "nonhumans" were also nonphysical in nature. The Dogon say that their teachers were concerned about the potentially detrimental effects that prolonged contact with them might have on us. The solution they arrived at for this problem was to sequester eight Dogon tribe members away from the tribe at some remote locale, provide them with civilizing instruction, then return them home again so that they could pass their newly acquired knowledge on to their compatriots. Dogon beliefs about the remote instruction of initiates are also echoed in the Buddhist tradition, which holds that knowledge was first imparted to humanity in ancient times at a remote location called Vulture Peak.

In *Point of Origin,* we discussed what outwardly appears to have been one of these remote instructional locales, an archaic mountaintop megalithic site in southeastern Turkey called Gobekli Tepe. Geographically speaking, Gobekli Tepe is situated in a region that is centrally located to Africa, Egypt, India, Tibet, and China, and it is so exceedingly ancient that its construction is estimated to have predated the earliest evidence we have for the tools required to build it. The site features a series of circular structures that, like those on Orkney Island, were built over time. They were composed of large stone pillars, stone benches, and stone walls whose functional purpose is poorly understood. What is known is that the site never served as an inhabited village, it has none of the design features of a military fortification, nor have human remains been found to suggest that it could have functioned as a burial site. Like Skara Brae, the structures seem to have been in active use for a period of centuries (perhaps upward of one thousand years) and then abandoned. But in the case of Gobekli Tepe, for reasons that are unknown, the structures are known to have been deliberately and carefully buried and so were preserved for posterity.

Stone for the pillars at Gobekli Tepe was excavated with skill from a quarry located some distance away and was transported to the site. Gobekli Tepe is located in the same general region as the Fertile Crescent, where we find the first evidence of cultivated grains, animal husbandry, and metallurgy. The pillars display artistically rendered images of birds and animals (sometimes carved in high relief), include a few anthropomorphized features such as arms, hands, and belts, and are marked with an occasional inscribed symbol. As the Buddhist term Vulture Peak might suggest, images of vultures are a prominent feature of that site. All outward signs support the idea that Gobekli Tepe could have been used as a remote instructional locale, comparable to what is claimed by the Dogon and Buddhists.

As part of our effort to understand the site, we explored ancient Egyptian names for the region of Turkey in which Gobekli Tepe is located, known in later eras as Cappadocia. Budge gives the Egyptian name as Getpetkai. Phonetically, the name Getpetkai is a close enough phonetic match to have conceivably survived (some twelve thousand years later) as Gobekli. Budge defines the name as an archaic form, and as such it may be subject to a different interpretive approach than the later Egyptian word forms we had worked with previously. The word begins with a glyph that is the image of a shrine and ends with a glyph that is understood to represent mountains. From these, we inferred that it could reasonably represent the name of a mountaintop shrine or sanctuary. The term led us to other geographical words in Budge's dictionary that, because they are similarly formulated, might also represent names for archaic sanctuaries.

Although the structures on Orkney Island seem to have been built many thousands of years later than Gobekli Tepe, both the island and its names suggest that it could have been conceived as a latter-day sanctuary of this same type—a locale for training initiates in skills of the same civilizing tradition and linked to the same cosmology. Both the nature of the Skara Brae village and its parallels to the Dogon Field of Arou lead us to believe that its primary focus would likely have been skills of agriculture, although clearly stone-working skills and skills of animal husbandry were also exercised there. From that perspective, the Egyptian three-plant glyph that Budge interprets as having represented reeds ⏸⏸⏸ might well have been meant to convey the image of cultivated seeds that grow into plants. This interpretation is supported by Dogon cosmological symbolism that links the Field of Arou to vibrations of matter and elemental particles, which are referred to metaphorically as "seeds."

From this perspective, the eight structures at Skara Brae might have served to house the eight members of each instructed "class" during their tenure as initiates at the site. In Dogon culture, it is specifically claimed that eight members of the tribe were sequestered together at a remote locale for instruction. Likewise, the presumed instructional focus on skills of agriculture might explain the remarked-on absence of fishing-related items among the artifacts excavated at the village.

Each civilizing skill of the Dogon was equated to a concept or process of cosmology. In our view, the structures along the road that led to

Skara Brae define those concepts of cosmological creation. On another level of symbolism, the Dogon skills were also linked to concepts of biological creation—the same essential biology that we see reflected in the ground plan of the Skara Brae houses. We understand the Dogon system to have descended from an archaic matriarchal cult whose focus was fertility. This outlook is also upheld in the ground plan of the Skara Brae house, which for the Dogon is conceptualized in relation to the body of a woman.

On yet another level of interpretation, the symbolic stages of creation define one meaning of the term *ascension,* which is a meaning that we associate with the archaic name for Orkney Island, Argat. In the Buddhist tradition, another perspective on the term *ascension* relates to a kind of energy of personal enlightenment that moves conceptually upward in the body from the region of the navel to the top of the head. Symbolically, a person's physical movement through the plan of the Skara Brae house would trace that same path of ascension.

As is the case for Gobekli Tepe, evidence suggests to some researchers that at the time that various structures of Skara Brae were abandoned, they were carefully, deliberately, and ritually buried, as if to preserve them for posterity.[1] Given that most societies simply abandon what is no longer deemed to be useful, this shared practice can be seen to constitute a ritual link between Skara Brae and the much earlier Gobekli Tepe site. Since no impending cataclysm or need to hide the structures from any apparently competitive group can be claimed as a motive for the Skara Brae practice, the implication is that this was done for ritualistic purposes, or as an intentional act of preservation.

In support of this view, our outlook is that the structures on Orkney Island (like the base plan of a Buddhist stupa or a Dogon granary) re-create the geometry by which creation emerges. One Dogon term for their granary is *ark,* and on one level the shrine symbolizes the eight wrapped-up dimensions of matter. The comparable Egyptian term is *arq,* and homonyms for this word cover a range of meanings that sensibly uphold the rationale of intentional preservation of the site. First, it means "to wrap up" or "to tie up."[2] As is true of the modern idioms "to wrap up" and "to tie up," the Egyptian term also means "to complete, to conclude, to finish, to make an end of." Significantly, the Egyptian word *arq* also means "to cover over." So from a strictly symbolic standpoint, covering the site indicates that the site's creators were finished with it and had concluded their process. More importantly, the term *arq,* meaning "to cover over," tells us what the site represented: an arq.

Discussion in *Point of Origin* shows that the eight incarnations of Ganesha also relate to these same eight dimensions of matter. Our outlook is that the archaic matriarchal tradition from India that celebrated Ganesha also influenced Egypt at the island of Elephantine in predynastic times. This implies that Hapy, the Egyptian god of the Nile who was worshipped at Elephantine, was a likely correlate to Ganesha. This viewpoint is upheld by another Egyptian word, *hap,* which also means "to cover over."[3]

Last but not least, there is an Egyptian word *suh* that also means "to cover over." It forms the phonetic root of a word *suhen,* which, for us, has ultimate significance for the Skara Brae site itself. It means "to overthrow."[4]

12

THE OVERTHROWN BOAT

Perhaps the signature theme of the system of cosmology we have been pursuing is given by the Hermetic phrase "as above, so below." This phrase reflects a central tenet of the tradition, which is that the processes of creation at work in the macrocosmic realm of the universe are in some way fundamentally similar to those that govern the microcosm, where matter forms. Many of the symbolic constructs of the ancient creation traditions can be seen as metaphors for this one theme.

For example, from one perspective of the tradition, the geometric shape of a circle is symbolically associated with processes of the macrocosm, which is referred to by the terms *heavens* and *above*. Similarly, the figure of a square relates to the processes of the microcosm, which is referred to by the terms *earth* and *below*. Knowing this, we can see that the notion of *squaring a circle* (essentially reconciling the shape and area of a circle with that of an equivalent square) can be taken to be symbolic of reconciling the processes of the heavens (above) with those of the earth (below). Likewise, we can understand that the figure of a hemisphere or a dome conceptually combines half a circle (above) with half a square (below) and so becomes a symbol for this same fundamental concept.

The egg of the world is defined by the Dogon priests as the critical structure on which matter is ostensibly based. It can be thought of as looking like a star with seven rays of increasing length, or it can be characterized by the spiral that can be drawn to inscribe those rays. Although the egg of the world is considered to be smaller than an atom, Dogon cosmological references point us to a macrocosmic counterpart of the egg that we identify with Barnard's Loop, a spiraling birthplace of stars located near the constellation of Orion. Barnard's Loop centers on the stars of Orion's Belt, and the Dogon priests refer to it as the Chariot of Orion.

Barnard's Loop emits such a small amount of light that it cannot be seen with the naked eye; however, it can be imaged using time-lapse photography. When we do image it, the red spiral of Barnard's Loop can be seen, and taken in context with the constellation of Orion, it gives the impression of the wheel of a chariot in which Orion the Hunter stands.

To bring these astronomical references into a more worldly frame, the archaic tradition used mythical storylines to essentially personify the structures. It can be argued that Barnard's Loop took the form of the Vedic god Siva, and the nearby bright star of Sirius played the role of his consort, the mother goddess Sati. In these myths, Sati created and gave life to a son, Ganesha the elephant, who symbolized the egg of the world and was cast in the cosmology as a kind of smaller counterpart to Siva.

In the ancient myth, one of Ganesha's first acts on behalf of his mother, whom he affectionately called Amma, was to act as a kind of gatekeeper for her while she bathes. The word *gatekeeper* is a cosmological term that refers to the thresholds between the seven wrapped-up dimensions of the egg of the world, and so it associates Ganesha with that structure. In *Point of Origin,* we discussed how the eight incarnations of Ganesha relate to the eight formative stages of the egg.

One essential characteristic of the two spirals represented by Siva and Ganesha is that they rotate, which produces a kind of vortex. The vortex of the smaller spiral, in the microcosm, is ostensibly responsible for the force of gravity. The larger spiral, in the macrocosm, causes the very slow rotation of the background stars that is called the cycle of precession.

These vortices are conceptual counterparts to swirling waterspouts in the ocean. In accordance with this comparison, Ganesha is traditionally said to have "emerged from the churning waters." One real-world effect of a swirling ocean waterspout is that it can overturn or capsize a ship at sea. In our view, the name Ganesha combines three smaller phonemes, the cosmological terms *ga, nu,* and *sa.* One definition of the Dogon term *ga* is "to overturn, as in water."[1] The comparable Egyptian term *gaa* means "to overturn" and is written with a glyph that is the image of a capsized boat 𓊐.[2] The Dogon and Egyptian words *nu* mean "water,"[3] and *sa* is an Egyptian word for "wisdom or knowledge deified."[4]

The Vedic god Siva (or Shiva) is sometimes referred to as "the destroyer." One implication within the cosmology is that periodically the vortex-like rotation of Barnard's Loop causes the magnetic field of the Earth to flip and, in so doing, essentially tips the Earth over like a capsizing boat. If that were to actually happen, the Earth would see widespread destruction, the ice caps would likely melt, and the magnetic poles would move to new regions. Large petrified forests in Antarctica, comparable to the primordial forests that Lewis and Clark found when they reached the West Coast of the United States, testify to the likelihood of this kind of event having occurred at some era in the past.

In our estimation, from a cosmological perspective the village of Skara Brae also represents the concept of the egg of the world. Appropriately, the Egyptian word *s-kher* means "overthrown."[5] If we are in doubt as to what Budge meant by the term *overthrow,* we can refer to his word entry for the word *pena,* which he gives as "to overthrow, to overturn, to capsize."[6] Likewise, the Egyptian word *bari* (a likely counterpart to the word *brae*) means "boat." From this perspective, the combined term Skara Brae (S-kher Bari) conveys the meaning of "overthrown boat." Appropriate to the Dogon symbolism for Barnard's Loop, which characterizes it as the Chariot of Orion, Budge includes a second word entry pronounced *bari* that means "chariot."[7]

These meanings, which seem justified in relation to egg-of-the-world symbolism, also seem justified by Skara Brae's positioning in relation to the structures of Orkney Island. They seem further justified in relation to the Greek myth of the journey of the Argonauts, whose boat, the *Argo* (named similarly to the term Argat), is said to have nearly capsized in the ocean at points along its way.

According to Marcel Griaule, the Dogon priests claim to be incapable of discussing a cosmological concept without also illustrating it at the same time. For this reason, they will often make a drawing in the sand or give reference to a familiar object to clarify the meanings of various cosmological concepts. When the Dogon priest Ogotemmeli began to explain the symbolism of the Dogon granary to Griaule, the priest searched around his living space for a woven basket to use as a conceptual aid. The basket was square on the bottom and had a slightly larger, round, open top. Turned upside down, it presented the same essential configuration as the one defined for the Dogon granary. Like the Buddhist stupa, this aligned shrine serves as a kind of grand mnemonic for Dogon cosmology. More specifically, the symbolism of the granary defines certain key creational stages of the egg of the world. Again appropriate to this symbolism, we learn from Budge's dictionary that the Egyptian word *bra*—another possible counterpart to the word *brae*—means "basket."[8] From that viewpoint, and apropos of Ogotemmeli's priestly metaphor, the name Skara Brae (S-kher Bra) could mean "overturned basket."

13

RECONSIDERING POSSIBLE ROLES FOR ORKNEY ISLAND

Our initial perspective when approaching the enigma of Skara Brae was to ask whether there might have been Egyptian influences on Orkney Island in ancient times. On reflection, however, and based on the types of evidence we have been discussing, we now see that this may have been an incorrect formulation of the question.

Traditional researchers see the period of 3200 BCE as having shortly preceded (by one or two hundred years) the dynastic period of ancient Egypt and the eventual unification of the Two Lands of Upper and Lower Egypt. From that perspective, the establishment of Skara Brae would have fallen into the predynastic (or what some researchers call the protodynastic) period of Egypt. This was an era during which, from all outward evidence, the ancient Egyptian culture was just beginning to take form. Given those considerations, it seems difficult to imagine anyone in Egypt having the mind-set, or luxury of time and resources, to reach out with a philanthropic expedition to the far reaches of the Western Ocean.

Moreover, the progression of structures we see on Orkney Island—those that are understood to have led by road directly to Skara Brae—reflect an informed and almost pedagogic influence, not that of an emerging culture. The suggestion is that these structures were formulated by someone who fully understood the symbology of cosmological creation and had mastered complex skills of stone working and farming. To the extent that the structures on Orkney Island reflect actual shapes that arise during the formation of matter (what the Buddhists call *adequate symbols*), they also imply intimate knowledge of the science that underlies the processes of creation.

Within the limits of our knowledge, none of this describes the predynastic culture of ancient Egypt. All outward signs are that, in this period, ancient Egypt was struggling to get on its feet. So the question arises as to whether the influences we are attempting to trace at Skara Brae might not, in actuality, have been the reverse of the ones we thought we were pursuing. What if, contrary to all expectations, Skara Brae had been the training ground for a pharaonic group that, in the period immediately following 3200 BCE, came to organize the structures of civilized society in dynastic Egypt?

This perspective implies the ongoing hand of knowledgeable ancestor-teachers on our planet across a period of several millennia. This group of teachers would have constituted the guiding influence behind the structures we find at Skara Brae, in much the same way that we believe they influenced the archaic sanctuary at Gobekli Tepe, thousands of years earlier. If we think about it, Egyptian and Buddhist nostalgia for a mythical First Time (an era of mythical instruction) actually implies that more than a single effort was made to convey that information, since the Egyptian reference is qualified to refer to the "first time" instruction occurred. The Buddhists similarly refer to "the first time knowledge was parted to humanity by a Buddha." The verbal construct implies more than one instance, much as Hebrew scholars assert that the admonition of the Jealous God to "have no other gods before me" implies the existence of prior gods. Perhaps the sanctuary-like structures we see on Orkney Island reflect a secondary effort to convey some of this same information, this time formulated in a somewhat different way.

The idea of a theoretical Secondary Time of instruction actually upholds evidence we see in various cultures of curious transitions in cosmological symbolism that occurred sometime between the archaic days of Gobekli Tepe and the First Dynasty of Egypt. For example, what was originally cast as a matriarchal tradition in Turkey, Iraq, and India later took its expression in Egypt, India, and elsewhere as a patriarchy. By dynastic times, it is the god Osiris whose body is dismembered and scattered, not the goddess Sati's.

The earliest traditions in India and China tell of a mother goddess who creates humanity from clay. In India it is Sati who breathes life into a clay doll she had made in order to produce a living son, while in China it is the goddess Nu-Wa who fashions man from clay. But by later times in many cultures, it is often a creator god who is credited with creating humanity from clay.

Similarly, the goddess Satet and her sister Anuket were celebrated at Elephantine at around 4000 BCE, but later these goddesses were supplanted by Hapy, the god of the Nile and of abundance. In early India, Ganesha's affectionate term Amma referred to his mother Sati, while in later eras, Amma is somewhat schizophrenically characterized as being "both male and female." In the later Dogon myths, Amma (like Amen in Egypt) is overtly cast as a creator god who performs a masturbatory act. The cross-cultural expression of these reversals in symbolism, all without outward cause in the same approximate era, reflects the effects of a cross-cultural influence.

Other comparable changes in symbolism can be seen to have occurred in various cultures sometime before the rise of dynastic Egypt. For example, archaic references that we assign to Barnard's Loop and that may have been originally tagged to the coiled tail of a mouse later seem to have been transferred to the similarly coiled trunk of an elephant. Symbolism that was at one time given in relation to two embracing elephants later was seemingly transferred to the Dogon nummo fish, where the word *nummo* overtly refers to a "perfect twin pair."

Such changes may have been introduced to recast certain symbols so that they aligned more intuitively with definitions of the cosmology in its mature form. For example, if the processes of creation were to be categorized in parallel with four classes of animals (insects, fish, four-legged animals, and birds), then the nonmaterial/material "embrace" that defines the Dogon egg of the world should have been given in relation to two fish, not two elephants. We know based on surviving myths from India that Ganesha's elephant's head was not deemed to have been his original head. We argued in *Point of Origin* that, based on linguistic references to the word *pen* or *penu,* the original symbolism may have aligned with an Egyptian shrew-mouse god. Based on that, Ganesha, who on one level seems to symbolize the spiral of Barnard's Loop, should properly be defined as an elephant (a large animal symbolizing a structure in the macrocosm), not as a mouse (an animal whose small size suggested the microcosm).

At about this same time, written language was introduced in places like ancient Egypt and was many times overtly credited as having been a gift from the gods. Among the written words of the language are what we take to be archaic forms (often correlated to Dogon words that are also traditionally understood to have been archaic) whose glyphs and pronunciations reflect a different symbolic (and sometimes phonetic) mind-set than that of later Egyptian hieroglyphic words. Many of these same transitions can be seen to have occurred during the same eras in various cultures and so again reflect the effects of some cross-cultural influence. Just as Osiris came to be emphasized over Isis in Egypt, Siva came to be emphasized over Sati in India.

Early archaic sanctuaries like Gobekli Tepe, which we interpret as instructional centers, were built in high mountaintop locations that presumably provided a degree of isolation and safety for any ancestor-teachers who might have been involved. On the other hand, the Orkney Island structures are positioned much closer to sea level and so could not have provided similar safety of distance or geographic inaccessibility. So the question arises as to what safe haven might have existed near Orkney Island to house a presumed group of ancestor-teachers. The obvious answer, based on their name, attributes, and geographic location, would be the nearby Faroe Islands, which are situated a short distance across the coastal waters of the Atlantic to the northwest of Orkney Island.

If this outlook is a correct one, we might expect to find that Egyptian concepts of "northwest" relate in some way to the notion of ancestor-teachers or the protection of ancestor-teachers. Budge lists a dictionary entry for "northwest" that is pronounced *mehti-amenti*.[1] *Meh* is an Egyptian word for "cubit," which implies the notion of measurement, and Amen is the Egyptian "hidden god." Budge defines the related word *mehtiu* to mean "gods of the north," and *mehti* to mean "north house."

The protective features of the Faroe Islands seem quite substantial, much grander in scale but comparable to those that made Alcatraz Island in San Francisco Bay the likely choice to locate a high-security prison. In an 1840 text titled *An Historical and Descriptive Account of Iceland, Greenland, and the Faroe Islands; with Illustrations of their Natural History,* an uncredited author describes the formidable protective aspects of the Faroe Islands:

The whole group [of islands] rises from the ocean, high and precipitous, surrounded by walls of lofty rocks, imposing on account of their wild aspect and deep bays and gulfs which separate them from each other. The cliffs, in many cases, are so perpendicular, that the boats are let down by ropes, whilst the sailors clamber up the sides by holes cut in the rocks. From the top of these walls, which are as smooth as if artificially built, a stone may be dropped into the sea 800 or 1000 feet below. . . . The extent of open sea on every side exposes Faroe to the full fury of the billows, which are broken by no sloping beach or shallows, the depth of water close to the shore being often so great that a ship may without difficulty touch the cliffs. The waves, even when excited by only a moderate breeze of wind, rise extremely high, dashing over the rocky promontories some hundreds of feet above the surface. The currents are also very remarkable . . . during stormy weather, there are often weeks and months during which it is impossible to pass from one island to another. . . . The tides and currents, meeting and forcing their way through the narrow channels amongst these islands, form several whirlpools, of which three are dangerous in high winds. . . . High winds . . . are extremely common, whirlwinds and hurricanes both in summer and winter being almost daily visitants . . . they inspire strangers with the utmost terror.[2]

The author goes on to say about one of the Faroe Islands called Kunoy, "Kunoe, to the north-west, is five miles long by two broad, and forms one continuous mountain, rising from the sea to the height of 2000 feet. The landing-places . . . on this [island] . . . are extremely dangerous, and boats are pulled up or let down by ropes."[3]

From this perspective, the rulers of dynastic Egypt, who would have been postured as agents of these godlike teachers, adopted the word *faro* (pharaoh) as the name of their place of residence and ultimately as a term of chieftainship, presumably as a way of emphasizing that their authority had been delegated from these ancestor-teachers. Traditional views of the Egyptian term for "pharaoh," *per-aa*, written as "structure" ☐ "of authority" ⟵,[4] are that it referred to a locality or structure where the person who symbolically held the scepter of authority lived. This seems consistent with our suggestion that the Faroe Islands might have served as a place of residence for a group of godlike authorities or teachers.

In support of this view of the Faroe Islands as a possible haven for godlike teachers of the pharaohs, the Egyptian word *per* means "house," "palace," or "seat of government,"[5] and the word *aa* can mean "island."[6] So there is a perspective from which the combined term *per-aa* could be interpreted to mean "home island," implying a seat of authority. The symbols of Budge's first spelling of the word for "island" read "that which" | "comes to be" 𓅱 "the cartouche" ▭.[7] A cartouche is the oval enclosure that, since around 2600 BC, was traditionally used to sur-

High, pyramid-like peaks in the Faroe Islands.
Photo: Vincent van Zeijst cc by-sa 3.0.

round the glyphs of the name of an Egyptian pharaoh. Prior to that era, these names were enclosed in a more rectangular *serekh* that is thought to have symbolized the facade of a palace. The change in usage appeared in Egypt at about the same time that the Orkney Island sites were abruptly abandoned. Alternately, Budge spells the word with a single glyph, the cartouche-shaped oval itself, the same figure that traditionally surrounds the inscribed name of a pharaoh. The suggestion is that the cartouche was meant to symbolize an island associated with the term *pharaoh*.

Budge also lists a related word, *aa-t*, which he defines as a name given to sections of the kingdom of Osiris, and a related term, *aat aakhu*, which refers to sections of the Sekhet Aaru[8] and which we take as a reference to the stone structures of the Orkney Island sanctuary.

This same term *per-aa*, or pharaoh, is arguably reflected as *faro* in the language of the Dogon and related cultures. However, as we noted in chapter 5, in the language of a related tribe called the Bambara, who share the Dogon cosmology, the term *faro* refers to the center point of the spiral of the egg of the world. Consequently, it also bears a relationship to Ganesha, whose incarnations define the egg of the world and whose traditional icons included the scepter. A similar and perhaps related Egyptian term is *per-abu,* which Budge defines as the Judgment Hall of Osiris. *Abu* is an Egyptian word for "elephant," and we take Osiris to be an Egyptian counterpart to the god Siva in India.

From the perspective of the archaic Sakti tradition, the term *per-aa* bears a likely relationship to the Hindu term *puran,* which forms the phonetic root of the name of a group of Hindu texts called the Puranas. From an Egyptian perspective, the word *puran* may combine the roots *per,* meaning "structure," and *an,* meaning "offering"—the same term that we associate with the cosmological structures that form what we see as the Field of Offerings on Orkney Island. The Devi Puran is the name of a Hindu text that describes the goddess Devi, who embodies the concept of the mother goddess and whose attributes reflect the cosmological "embrace" of the material and nonmaterial universes. There is also a perspective from which the term *sakti* (pronounced *shakti*) itself associates with the notion of an instructed system of agriculture. In India, it is understood that the term *sakti* combines two phonetic roots: *sha* and *kti.* In Egypt, the word *sha* can mean "field," and the word *kheti* means "measure," which implies the notion of a cubit, the traditional unit by which agricultural fields were measured out.

Another Egyptian word for "island" or "land close to a river" is *ma-t.*[9] The cosmological concept of a primeval mound, which we believe to be symbolized by Maes Howe, is alternately described as a kind of island within a sea of primordial waves. *Maat,* of course, is the name for the underlying Egyptian principle of truth, authority, balance, and justice, which it is the pharoah's job to uphold. Maa was an Egyptian god and Maat an Egyptian goddess of this same principle.

Another Egyptian word for "island" was *nemai.*[10] This word calls to mind the Dogon term *nummo,* which (on one level) the Dogon priests applied to their ancestor-teachers. For the Dogon, both the teachers and the term *nummo* also had intimate associations with water. The Egyptian term *nemma* means "to build or construct," skills that we see evidenced by the stone structures on Orkney Island.[11]

Archaeologists who are familiar with Orkney Island tell us that the structures at Skara Brae were only in use for a period of about six hundred years, up until around 2600 BCE. This suggests that Greeks such as Homer, Pindar, and Virgil, who lived in a later era, could not have had direct experience with the structures during the instructional era and so likely learned about them (and perhaps about the island of Orkney itself) from the Egyptian priests. Just as modern archaeologists interpret Maes Howe as having been a burial cairn for dignitaries, Greek legends of the Elysian Fields tell us that heroes were buried there, near to the gods. Once again, the implication is that the ancestor-teachers were understood to have been located near Maes Howe, and this understanding would seem to have been communicated to the Greeks by the Egyptians.

Variations we have seen in the pronunciation of cosmological terms from region to region provide us with a method for tracing the likely lineage of specific influences. For example, in *Point of Origin,* when discussing relationships between incarnations of Ganesha in India and the Dogon egg of the world, or po pilu, I linked the Dogon word *pilu* to Turkish and Tamil words (the language of the Dravidians) that mean "elephant." That, along with other evidence, conforms to our view that the Dogon tradition descended from Turkey, through the Dravidians and the Sakti cult in India, to Egypt and then to Mali in West Africa. This outlook is supported by Dogon designations for their creator god Amma, who has a feminine aspect, and so aligns in India both with Ganesha's Amma, as he called Sati, and with a related Dravidian form of the mother goddess called Uma. Modern perspectives on Amma as the creator god of the Dogon affirm the apparent reversals in symbolism discussed previously in this chapter.

The Turkish word for "elephant," like the Faroese word, is pronounced *fil.* That would make sense if the word originated as *fil* with the ancestor-teachers in Turkey and then simply retained its form when it was expressed centuries later in the Faroe Islands by that same ancestral group. In Hebrew, the word for "elephant" is pronounced *pil*. However, the complex grammar of the Hebrew language creates situations in which the word could also conceivably be pronounced *fil*. These situations relate to archaic phonemes such as those that, in *Point of Origin*, we suggested survived in India pronounced as *g* but in Egypt pronounced as *h*. Seven such complex phonemes are understood to exist in the Hebrew language.

Differences in the pronunciations *pil* and *fil* are seemingly reconciled in the Hebrew language in relation to the letters *pey* and *fey*, which are pronounced like the English letters *P* and *F*. The cursive versions of these letters are written as a spiral around a central dot, comparable to the spiral of the Dogon egg of the world and the "twisted trunk" figure we associated with the first incarnation of Ganesha in *Point of Origin*.

In overview, all of these points of evidence support the idea that a pre-Vedic matriarchal tradition centered on the mother goddess Sati and a counterpart to her elephant-headed son Ganesha expressed its influence in Upper (southern) Egypt at Elephantine by around 4000 BCE. Here, the sister goddesses Satet and Anuket were celebrated. In the Sakti tradition of India, counterparts to these sister goddesses were always attended in art by their son, the elephant-headed Ganesha, one of whose titles meant "he who has two mothers." From that perspective, the Egyptian Nile god Hapy, who was also celebrated at Elephantine, could be a likely counterpart to Ganesha.

Elephantine was also home to the oldest Jewish temple in ancient Egypt. One likely Egyptian name for the likely builders of this temple was given by Budge as Habiru, perhaps a correlate to the modern term Hebrew, and referred to a group of stone masons, who wore aprons known as *apiru*. However, the cosmological symbolism suggests that the term might well have been given in relation to the Egyptian god Hapy and so might possibly have originated as Hapy Ru, meaning "kingdom of Hapy" symbolized by a lion, whose Egyptian name was Ru. In support of that view, the other primary Egyptian locale that celebrated Hapy was Gebel el Silsila, an archaic stone quarry not far down the Nile River from Elephantine that provided construction material for many of the magnificent temples of ancient Egypt.

From that same perspective, at around 3100 BCE, the faros, or pharaohs, whom we see as initiates of the Secondary Time instruction at Orkney Island, would have arrived in Lower (northern) Egypt with an imperative to establish a civilization based on agriculture and a now increasingly patriarchal reformulation of the originally matriarchal cosmological tradition. This difference in outlook (patriarchal versus matriarchal) between the earlier and later instructed traditions may have provided a means by which the ancestor-teachers could trace the relative influence and effectiveness of two separate attempts at instruction. That would be consistent with a ritual of circumcision that may have been instituted in order to tag the migrations of adherents to the original cosmology. By the time of Pharoah Narmer, or Menes, the Two Lands (Upper and Lower Egypt) are thought to have been unified, and the earlier matriarchal tradition would have begun to be replaced by the more modern patriarchal system that ultimately came to define ancient Egypt.

14
THE EMERGENCE OF DYNASTIC EGYPT

Toby A. H. Wilkinson writes in *Early Dynastic Egypt* that the history of Egypt began at Abydos. Abydos was situated roughly midway along the Nile between the delta and Elephantine, the locale that in *Point of Origin* I associated with goddesses of the Sakti tradition, which also links to the goddess Sati, her son Ganesha, and the god Siva. At around 3100 BCE, during what is considered to be the late predynastic period (some researchers refer to this period, somewhat misleadingly, as Dynasty 0, since it preceded what has come to be known as the First Dynasty in Egypt), a king named Ka appears. His name, which is found on ceramic artifacts, is written with two arms—the same image that we associate with the archaic matriarchal tradition at Gobekli Tepe.

In his dictionary, Budge defines the term *ka*, written ⌴ 𓂓 , as the name of a deity or deified concept, which he describes as "the father of the fathers of the gods."[1] Budge notes that this is equivalent to the concept expressed by the glyphs ⌣𓏤 ⌣𓏤 𓄤.[2]

The image of the collective vessel that defines Budge's reference is pronounced like the English letter *k* and, in Budge's estimation, is an equivalent for ⌣𓏥, which we interpret to mean "collective existence"—one effective definition for a civilized nation-state such as dynastic Egypt. However, the word is actually written with two such collective-vessel glyphs, which are inscribed physically above and below one another. The suggestion is that two "collective existences" were actually established at the onset of dynastic times, one as Upper Egypt and the other as Lower Egypt. We take these Two Lands to be symbolic both of the cosmological phrase "as above, so below" and of two universes (nonmaterial and material) whose existences are effectively linked to one another in our archaic tradition.

The third glyph in the term that Budge equates with the deified concept of ka is the image of the overthrown boat ⟨glyph⟩, which is familiar to us from our discussions of Skara Brae. From our perspective, the relationship of this image to the name Skara Brae (which we interpret as S-kher Bari) constitutes a signature that carries us conceptually back to the sanctuary on Orkney Island. We have mentioned here and in *Point of Origin* that the concept of rotation as it relates to the spiral of the Dogon egg of the world and to Barnard's Loop is also compared to a capsized boat. This relationship is established through the symbols of Egyptian words and by overt definition in the Dogon dictionary. The overthrown boat image might also suggest the reversal in maternal/paternal symbolism that seemingly began to take effect in Egypt at around the time of the establishment of dynastic kingship.

Like the deified concept of ka, the name of the king Ka was also written with the dual-handed glyph ⟨glyph⟩. The image of the glyph is a correlate to the disembodied carved arms and hands that wrap around the ends of a pillar at the mountaintop sanctuary of Gobekli Tepe in Turkey. From our perspective, the two arms symbolize the concept of a motherly embrace and depict an entwined, almost parental link between a nonmaterial universe and our material universe. As such, the arms constitute one of the quintessential symbolic images of the archaic cosmological tradition.

For Budge, the term *ka* also implies the concepts of personal character, disposition, and vital strength that defined the role of the pharaoh in ancient Egypt.[3] In addition, we see from Budge's word entries that the phoneme implies the notion of "another" that inheres in the concept of a collective existence.

Budge lists one name for Elephantine, *Abu,* which is spelled with glyphs that read "scepter's" "place" "of the elephant" , followed by the three-humped mountain glyph that, for us, defines the Egyptian names of archaic sanctuaries.[4] Elephantine was home to a series of archaic sanctuaries that we link to Sakti-like mother goddesses and to the Egyptian god Hapy, whom we interpret as a likely counterpart to Ganesha. The scepter is an icon both of Ganesha in India and of kingship in Egypt. Budge gives the name of Abydos, where the kingship of Ka was established, as Abt. It is based on a phonetic root *aab,* which means "scepter."[5] Another Egyptian term, *aab-t,* means "the east."[6] We interpret one spelling for the name of Abydos as "scepter's" "place" "of matters" "civic" .[7] The implication is that Elephantine was established primarily as a religious sanctuary, while Abydos was understood to be primarily a seat of government. The term "east" implies a point of reference for the meaning that lay somewhere west of Egypt.

The idea that the establishment of dynastic kingship at Abydos might have been associated with major revisions in the cosmology is supported by the eventual rise in significance there of the Egyptian god Osiris, a Lower Egyptian deity who had been known since ancient times.[8] Certain cosmological myths associated with Osiris, such as the story of his death, dismemberment, and resurrection, have obvious correlates in the Sakti tradition but are given there in relation to the mother goddess Sati, not Osiris's likely Vedic male counterpart deity, Siva. Likewise, the names and roles of the characters in the Sakti myth make the cosmological aspects of the tale fairly obvious, while Osiris's cosmological role remains less apparent. The Egyptian mother goddess Neith has known roots in the predynastic era. Other familiar Egyptian deities such as the sun god Ra rose to prominence only after the start of the dynastic period.

We have said that in early dynastic times, the inscribed name of a pharoah was enclosed not by an oval cartouche, but rather by a more rectangular *serekh.* Ostensible examples of a serekh inscribed in proximity with presumed names of kings have been dated to late predynastic times, but associations between the two are speculative. The Egyptian word *serekh* actually means "throne," an object that was a signature icon of the Egyptian goddess Isis and was also associated mythically with Sati and other mother goddesses in India. The word *serekh* shares a phonetic root with the Egyptian word *s-rekh*, meaning "to make to know,"[9] which implies the concept of teaching. Both meanings link to aspects of the archaic traditions that I discussed in *Point of Origin*.

Also, by our standard of interpretation, the glyphs of the term *s-rekh* symbolically define the meaning of its unpronounced trailing glyph, which in this case is the Sphinx-like head and paws of a lion . The traditionally acknowledged antiquity of the Sphinx suggests that this surely represented an archaic symbol. If the intention at 3100 BCE was to supplant the symbolism of an archaic matriarchal tradition with newly cast patriarchal references, then the adoption of the oval cartouche in place of the serekh makes sense as part of that effort.

When discussing the stone structures at Skara Brae in chapter 4, we offered a comparison between the plan of the earliest houses built at Skara Brae and the very similar plan of a typical house in Dogon society. These both featured a round "beehive" room that represented a woman's head, a rectangular main room that served to symbolize her main body cavity, and a rectangular entryway that symbolized her sexual parts or vulva. Similar symbolism that relates both to a woman and to a house also characterized cult shrines in early dynastic Egypt. Because these shrines were built from perishable materials rather than stone, physical examples have not survived. However, representations of these shrines are given on ancient tablets and cylinder seals. Byron E. Shafer of Fordham University writes in *Temples of Ancient Egypt*, "The reed shrines are larger versions of domestic huts. Their cultic function is clear, for depicted at the entrance of the enclosure are two poles with banners. This symbol was later used in hieroglyphs for the word *ntr* [neter], meaning 'god' or 'divine.' . . . The gateway probably symbolized the vagina and (re)birth . . . [and] led inward to the womblike sanctuary of the principal god."[10]

In keeping with the patriarchal outlook of later dynastic Egypt, Shafer interprets the symbolism of these shrines as having related primarily to a god. However, it seems clear that interpreted meanings that pertain to a vagina and a womb must have originally been given in relation to a mother goddess and so uphold the view that reversals in symbolism occurred.

Additional support for our outlook of likely connections between Skara Brae house symbolism and that of structures of early dynastic Egypt is upheld by the very similar plan of early burial sites in ancient Egypt. The image on the opposite page, which represents an "elite" First Dynasty burial chamber, replicates these same three rooms, which are defined in the Dogon architectural plan as the "main house."

Supportive of this outlook, Budge includes a word for "grave" that is pronounced *an*, alongside a word for "abode" that is pronounced *an-t*.[11] Other Egyptian words for "grave" can be seen as homonyms for actions that would be performed in a house, such as slumbering and eating.

The numerous clay pots that were found to fill one of the chambers of the "house" at Minshat Abu Omar call to mind symbolic offerings called potbellies—clay pots filled with water that symbolized wombs and were associated with the mother goddess in archaic times. Toby A. H. Wilkinson of the University of Durham writes in *Early Dynastic Egypt*, "The ancient royal necropolis of Abydos—more specifically, the area known by its modern Arabic name Umm el-Qaab (literally 'mother of pots,' from the vast quantities of offering pottery littering the site)—was the focus of royal burials throughout the First Dynasty, and again at the end of the Second Dynasty."[12]

If we believe what the Dogon priests assert as fact, the primary purpose of the archaic civilizing plan was to raise the status of humanity from the level of hunter-gatherers to the level of farmers. From that perspective, the establishment of kingship in Egypt, in conjunction with a self-sustaining system of agriculture, would mark the practi-

An "elite" First Dynasty burial site at Minshat Abu Omar.
By permission of Staatliches Museum Agyptischer Kunst Munchen.

cal accomplishment of that goal. We see this outlook reflected in one Egyptian word for "throne," which Budge pronounces *uthes-t*.[13] The term is based on the phonetic root *uthes,* which means "to lift up, to support, to raise."[14] In turn, both words rest on the phoneme *uth,* which means "reed," the same term that we associate with cultivated plants on Orkney Island. Symbolically, the word *uth* reads "the established" "existence" "of agriculture" .

In his book *Ancient Egypt: Anatomy of a Civilization*, Barry J. Kemp of Cambridge University attributes the formation of the dynastic state in ancient Egypt largely to the existence of a stable agriculture. He writes, "Egypt is particularly interesting because, apart from being one of the earliest examples, state formation seems to have taken place in the absence of some of the more obvious factors. . . . The dynamic for the growth of the state seems in many instances to lie inherent within the very fact of settled agriculture."[15]

Budge defines a deity named Uteth as a form of Thoth,[16] who was considered the Lord of the Divine Words and who was celebrated at Abydos alongside a female counterpart named Seshat. (Interestingly, some sources equate Seshat with Nephthys, the sister of Isis, and with the goddess Anuket, who was the sister of the Sati-like goddess Satet celebrated at Elephantine.[17]) The name Uteth can be interpreted symbolically to read "growth of" 🐦 "the material" ⌓ "in concert with" ▭ "the spiritual/nonmaterial" 🦅, followed by the Horus falcon glyph, which we interpreted in *The Cosmological Origins of Myth and Symbol* to signify the concept of a symbol, based on its usage in Egyptian words that mean "symbol" 🦅.[18] The falcon was also a symbol of kingship in Egypt. It is of interest that similar falcons are also native to the Orkney Island region.

Budge also defines the term Uthes-hehtt, which takes the form of the name of a sanctuary. The term itself includes the phoneme *het,* meaning "temple or sanctuary," and the trailing determinative is our familiar three-humped mountain glyph ⌒⌒⌒. Comparable to the Elysian Fields concept, Budge considers this to have been "the country of resurrection." The term Uthes-neferu refers to "the name of a sacred boat of Ra" and includes the upright boat as its final determinative ⛵.[19] The implication is that one beneficial effect on humanity of civilizing instruction from godlike teachers was essentially to "right" the overthrown boat. Altogether, this perspective on the concept of a throne seemingly touches on each of the pertinent symbolic elements we find on Orkney Island and at Skara Brae while also upholding our theoretical rationale for the establishment of dynastic Egypt.

Stephen Quirke tells us in his book *Ancient Egyptian Religion* that from earliest dynastic times in Egypt, there was a temple at Abydos near where the first kings were buried that was dedicated to Khentamentiu, the "foremost of the Westerners."[20] He interprets this as a reference to the dead and suggests that the term might refer to all of the previously deceased predynastic kings. Budge lists the word *khenti-amentiu,* which he defines to mean "first of those in Amenti," a reference to a title of

Osiris.[21] The Egyptian word *khenti* refers to a forerunner or leader, "he who is at the head." It is based on a root, *khent,* that, like the Scottish term *ness,* means "nose." Also like the Scottish word *ness,* it can refer to "any prominent place, point, tip or limit."[22]

The word *amenti,* which based on Budge's usage must refer to a place, is based on the Egyptian word *amen,* which means "to hide, to conceal, to be hidden, secret mysterious."[23] The word *ament* refers to "the West" and "the abode of the dead,"[24] but it also can be defined in terms of "a hidden place" or "sanctuary." The word *amenti* refers to "a denizen of Amen-t, one belonging to Amen-t." So the implication is that the title *khenti-amentiu* might actually refer to "the foremost of those at a secret Western sanctuary" and reasonably a sanctuary that was associated with the dead. From this perspective, the Old Kingdom temple at Abydos would have been dedicated to the leaders of the sanctuary on Orkney Island.

Budge tells us that the Egyptian word *amen-t* also is the "name of a sceptre amulet," based on a phonetic root *amen* that means "to establish."[25] The scepter, of course, was a symbol of the establishment of culture and kingship in Egypt, and Amen was an Egyptian counterpart to the Dogon creator god Amma. The Faroese and Icelandic term *kenna* means "teach," and the Faroese term *mentan* (comparable to the Icelandic word *menning*) means "culture."[26] If we were to allow that perspective, the term *khenti-amentiu* might be interpreted to mean "teachers of culture."

Quirke also says that perhaps the most impressive monument at Abydos was a symbolic grave of Osiris, constructed during the New Kingdom in Egypt by Seti I and his son Rameses II. He says it was "sunk low in the sand behind his temple, with water around a central island to which a sloping corridor descends as if to the underworld itself."[27] It is interesting that Quirke's description of the monument repeats the configuration and symbology of the Neolithic low road on Orkney Island itself.

15

THE ADVENT OF
THE EGYPTIAN
HIEROGLYPHS

There is an ancient tradition that the written hieroglyphic language was given to the Egyptians by their gods. In the context of the Secondary Time instruction that we are entertaining, it becomes possible to demonstrate the likelihood of that claim. The argument to support this outlook takes shape in several stages. First, we know that although Dogon culture preserves many of the words, symbols, and practices of ancient Egypt as they may have existed in earliest times, it did not preserve an actual written language. Marcel Griaule's view was that it would be unthinkable that the Dogon once had a written language but had since forgotten it. Since multiple points of evidence seem to place Dogon involvement with the Egyptians at around 3200 BCE, the indication is that the Egyptians also had no written language prior to dynastic times. Based on artifacts discovered to date, the earliest written Egyptian texts support that outlook.

Given this, the mere fact that we encounter archaic word forms in the Egyptian hieroglyphic language introduces a somewhat confusing and contradictory situation. If our view is that the Egyptian hieroglyphic language made its first appearance at around 3100 BCE, it is reasonable to think that the Dogon and Egyptians could share archaic phonetic words. But in that context, how can it be possible for the Egyptian word to be given in a written form that is also deemed to be archaic?

In *Point of Origin,* we discussed some of these archaic words, along with the phonetic and written forms they take. In some cases, Egyptian words that we deem to be archaic are also overtly designated as archaic by Genevieve Calame-Griaule in her *Dictionnaire Dogon.* Given that, we would seem to be on firm ground in suggesting a common Dogon and Egyptian lineage for these words, one that seems to reach back to the Tamil and Turkish words that characterize the Sakti cult and our discussions of Gobekli Tepe.

Since, in the absence of a written language, the Dogon words are purely phonetic, the sets of discrete meanings that attach to the words represent multiple definitions of a single word. In the Egyptian hieroglyphic language, these same meanings can be expressed with configurations of glyphs that differ from one another but are pronounced similarly and so give the impression of *homonyms* in English—words that are pronounced alike but spelled differently. In an Egyptian text, when the homonym of an arguably intended word appears (perhaps to deliberately obscure the true meaning of the text), modern researchers often interpret the usage as a pun.

When we apply our interpretive method of reading later Egyptian hieroglyphic words, we substitute concepts for the glyphs of the word to produce a kind of symbolic sentence that defines the word's meaning. Sometimes an unpronounced trailing glyph is also attached to the word, and in those cases we assign that same sentence's meaning to the trailing glyph. The word essentially defines one symbolic interpretation for the trailing glyph. A good example of this convention is illustrated by the Egyptian word *am,* which means "to grasp." It is written:

"to come" 🦅 "to know" 🦅,
followed by the grasping-fist glyph 🖐[1]

By contrast, archaic Egyptian words employ apparent conventions of writing that can be outwardly quite different from those of the more familiar words of dynastic Egypt. In some cases the archaic words are written with two or more introductory glyphs and then seem to simply define their own meanings pictorially with one or more glyphs whose images illustrate the word's definition. As examples of this archaic method, we have the Egyptian word *ga,* meaning "bull," which is written as:

We also have the archaic word *gaa,* meaning "to overturn," written as:

With this example, we once again see that in an Egyptian word for "overturn," the notion of overturning is illustrated with the image of an overthrown boat. Budge notes that this word for "overturn" is a perceived pun on an archaic word whose symbols read:

"that which is" | "authority's" | "standard" |

Given the role we propose for Skara Brae in the establishment of dynastic kingship in Egypt, it seems significant that Budge's acknowledged relationship between these two words overtly links the symbol of the scepter of kingship to the concept of an overturned boat.

As Budge notes, the proper phonetic value assigned to some glyphs may have been different in archaic times than in historic times, which would mean that certain words could have been pronounced differently, too. This feature of the language accounts for archaic sanctuary names like Getpetkai that were originally given in relation to the phoneme *get* (implying "house," "temple," or "sanctuary") but re-created later for counterpart temples in Egypt as *het.*

What these differences imply is that symbolic written language may also have gone through a significant reformulation at around the same time as the myths, deities, and cosmology. If so, then archaic Egyptian words would represent the language (unknown to modern researchers) as it may have existed in relation to the archaic tradition, while the more familiar historic Egyptian hieroglyphs would represent the language after its reformulation.

However, there is very little archaeological evidence of an archaic tradition of writing in Egypt prior to 3000 BCE, and the lack of written language among the Dogon argues that no such formal tradition existed in predynastic Egypt. So if the hieroglyphs we see in Egypt at 3000 BCE represent a reformulation of the symbolic written language, where should we presume to say the system of writing was originally formulated? The suggestion is that the written language was originally developed by the ancestor-teachers sometime after 10,000 BCE, reformulated in the Faroe and Orkney Islands along with the Secondary Time cosmology, and then instituted in Egypt hand in hand with pharaonic rule. In other words, it would be as the ancient Egyptians profess it to have been: the hieroglyphic system of writing was given to them by their ancestor-teachers.

Our understanding of the Dogon culture suggests that the cosmology began as a nonliterate tradition and was passed down orally from generation to generation. Given the very effective mnemonic nature of the symbols and rituals of the cosmology, this viewpoint makes sense. Concepts of the cosmology were also expressed in relation to specific phonetic values. For example, the phoneme *si* implied Sirius, *ra* referred to the sun, and *am* represented the concept of knowledge. These phonemes defined basic conceptual building blocks, and more complex cosmological concepts were assembled from the phonemes by grouping them in combination with one another. Knowing this and the correct concepts to associate with each phoneme, a person can reasonably predict the meaning of a cosmological term simply based on its pronunciation. For example, if *nu* represents the concept of water or waves, and *ma* represents the concept of perception, then the compound term *nu maa* implies the notion of "waves perceived."

These phonemes laid a foundation for defining the terms of

cosmology. But it also seems clear that foundations for eventual written language were set in place as early as 10,000 BCE. We argue that the carved images of animals found on pillars at Gobekli Tepe represented a kind of protowriting. The Egyptian name for each animal pictured on the Gobekli Tepe pillars is pronounced like a key term of the cosmology. The suggestion is that a hunter-gatherer would see the carved image on a pillar, say the familiar name of the animal, and essentially speak a cosmological term that he or she could then associate with an instructed concept.

Serge Sauneron states in *The Priests of Ancient Egypt* that it was true in all eras of ancient Egyptian culture that, for the Egyptian priests, mere similarity of pronunciation implied a relationship between two words. Marcel Griaule holds the same to be true for the Dogon. Traces of these same archaic phonemes can be found in the languages of other cultures. In our experience, the more ancient and historically isolated the language, the more likely it is that we will find phonemes of the cosmology associated with appropriate cosmological concepts. In cases like the Faroese language, where Scandinavian influences are known to have intermixed with an ancient language for thousands of years, it is understandable that a modern Faroese dictionary reveals only intermittent matches to the cosmological phoneme-concept relationships we anticipate. The same is true for modern-day Turkish- and Tamil-language dictionaries.

16
CORRELATING REGIONAL KINGSHIPS AT 3000 BCE

In our outlook on the roots of pharaonic rule in Egypt, the establishment of dynastic kingship served as a finalizing stage in the instructed system of agriculture that defines the archaic civilizing plan. Through this act (the implementation of a self-sustaining state) a major educational step was achieved, civilization could be said to have taken root, and the primary goals of the civilizing plan would have been accomplished. Support for this view is found in the Egyptian word for "king," which Budge pronounces *suten*. (He notes in his dictionary entry that "in the Early Empire the reading [of the word] . . . was *nesu*."[1]) The term *nes/ness* is one that we associate with the locales of Orkney Island and Scotland. In Egypt, the word *nes* implies a concept of authorized ownership that rises to the level of legal property. The Dogon term *su* refers to an agreement. In light of those definitions, the combined term *nesu* would imply kingship that was delegated from an authority by legal agreement. Symbolically, the word *suten* reads "agriculture" ⸙ "established" △ ∿∿∿ . In other contemporaneous cultures we have studied, such as ancient China, a primary accomplishment that is attributed to the earliest mythical kings is the establishment of agriculture. By comparison, the Dogon have no documented word for "king" but only have a term for chieftainship that they pronounce *faro*.

To all outward appearances, Orkney Island served as a kind of pre-dynastic instructional center, and its apparent focus was primarily on agriculture. The pastoral farming life that clearly thrived for centuries on the island bore a relationship to the cosmology enshrined there that is similar to the one borne by dynastic Egyptian culture to its comparable creation tradition, which the Egyptians also felt compelled to enshrine in stone. In prior books of this series, we have correlated many different aspects of Dogon civic life, religion, and language to likely counterparts in ancient Egypt. So, to the extent that Dogon culture accurately reflects elements of life found at Skara Brae, then by a transitive property we might interpret Skara Brae to have been a kind of model for early Egyptian farming culture.

From this perspective, we suggest that Orkney Island represented the real-world incarnation of the Egyptian Sekhet-Aaru, or Field of Reeds, a term that, based on both Dogon references and Egyptian glyph images, we interpret to represent the concept of a cultivated field. However, there are further complexities to the Egyptian term *aaru,* a word that Budge defines to mean "reeds."[2] When we examine Budge's dictionary entry for the word, we notice that one of his spellings for the word is given with a single glyph, one that presents the image of a hemispheric sun with rays emitting from it ☀.[3] This glyph is a close correlate to a carved figure found at Newgrange, a prehistoric passage tomb in Ireland that is estimated to have been constructed in the same era as Skara Brae, also at around 3200 BCE ☼.[4] In other words, there is a perspective from which the term *aaru,* which we associate with Orkney Island, might also reasonably apply to Ireland, and perhaps even to the larger domain of Great Britain.

This outlook seems sensible when we consider that an ancient name for Ireland was Eire, a term that bears a phonetic resemblance to the Dogon and Egyptian phonemes *ar* or *aar,* and that an Egyptian term for "lion" (which is also an ancient symbol associated with Ireland) is *ru.*[5] Furthermore, in Egypt Aaru was the name of the god of the Field of Reeds, and from our perspective on Egyptian hieroglyphs, the symbols of the word define the lion glyph .[6] Terms for "lion," such as the Hebrew word *arye,* were based on similar phonetic roots in numerous ancient cultures. Looked at in this way, the term *aaru* could reasonably imply the meaning of Lion of Eire, or Ireland.

In addition to this, we know it is clear that, from archaic times, the lion was also an identifying symbol of ancient Egypt. One Egyptian word for the Sphinx at Giza, pronounced *hu,* is actually written with a lion glyph.[7] Likewise, we know that the lion is an animal that has been traditionally associated with kingship in many different societies. So the suggestion is that the term *aaru* as we understand it in relation to Ireland might well have pertained to kingship and so constituted the archaic name of a regional kingdom.

Knowing this, it is interesting that Egyptian texts preserve the following detail: the god Osiris, upon arriving at Abydos, is quoted as having referred to the province of Abydos as the "great land," or Tawer.[8] Given the context of our discussion and knowing that the pronunciation of ancient Egyptian words is not certain (as with ancient Hebrew, vowel sounds were only inferred, not written), we interpret the term Tawer as a sensible correlate for the (in our estimation) likelier term *taru.* This word, which we also take as the name of a regional kingdom (in this case, dynastic Egypt seated at Abydos), takes the same form as the term *aaru* and reflects similar lion symbolism as we propose for the term in Ireland. In short, from these two words we infer the contours of yet another potential naming convention of our cosmological tradition—one in which regional kingships established as an outgrowth of Secondary Time instruction on Orkney Island took predictable name forms that combined a leading two-character phoneme with the term *ru,* which expressed the implied notion of "lion," "king," or "kingdom."

If we entertain this naming convention as a valid interpretation, then we would expect to find other regional kingdoms from the same era whose names follow the same general pattern. The first obvious example of a contemporaneous culture known for megalithic construction and high mountaintop sanctuaries comparable to those in the archaic tradition could be Peru, in South America. Evidence of monumental architecture, systematized agriculture, and organized civil states are found along the coast of Peru and date to the same approximate time period as early dynastic Egypt.[9] Budge says that the Egyptian term *peru* refers to "men attached to the royal granary."[10] The term *granary* is one that carries important symbolism for our cosmology and plays an obviously important role in agriculture and so satisfies both of the conceptual themes we see reflected on Orkney Island.

Another regional kingdom that might be a likely candidate for this same naming convention is ancient China, where the lion again served as a known symbol of kingship. The term *yiru*, or *iru*, is an archaic name that we associate with China. *Yi* (pronounced *eee*) represents the concept of transformation or change-in-state that is defined by the *Yijing*, or *I-Ching*. In the Dogon language, the term *iru* refers to grain, which we take to mean a crop growing in a field. It also refers to the smithy who fashions the metal tools of agriculture. Cosmologically, this smithy plays a Prometheus-like role in a Dogon myth in which he steals fire from the gods for use in his forge. The forge of the smithy is then housed on the roof of the granary. Here we can see that the term *iru* reflects themes of cosmology and agriculture, along with the notion of an arguably assisted establishment of agriculture.

This viewpoint is supported by the existence in ancient China of a system of agricultural land use called the well-field system, which is a direct match for Dogon agricultural practices, and which we discuss in *China's Cosmological Prehistory*. The concept in both societies was to establish squared plots consisting of nine smaller squares, three per side. In theory, eight of these plots were assigned to individual families to cultivate for their own benefit, supported by a shared well that stood in the ninth center plot. In actual practice, despite the reticence of many modern academics to endorse the legitimacy of the form, variations on this plan were eventually implemented. However, some researchers believe the system to have been purely theoretical in China and never actually implemented. In the archaic Dogon version of this plan, which is understood to be legitimate, plots of varying size were laid out in the shape of a spiral, mimicking the spiral associated with the egg of the world in Dogon cosmology.

If our outlook is correct, these four comparably named regional kingships seem to symbolically reflect four stages in the processes of agriculture. These would be:

Taru (Egypt) = earth to be cultivated
Aaru (Ireland) = a cultivated field
Yiru/Iru (China) = grain growing in the field
Peru (Peru) = harvested grain stored in a granary

Cosmologically, the kingships would also seem to reflect the four primordial elements as they were later known to the Greeks:

Taru (Egypt) = earth
Aaru (Ireland) = water (required to cultivate a field)
Yiru/Iru (China) = wind (blows through a field of grain)
Peru (Peru) = fire (housed in the forge of the granary)

From this same cosmological perspective, these four elements symbolize stages in the formation of matter, but the terms play out in a slightly different sequence:

Water represents matter in its wavelike state.
Fire represents an act of perception.
Wind represents the concept of vibration.
Earth represents the concept of mass or matter.

Support for the notion that four regional kingships, founded on a self-sustaining system of agriculture and symbolized by lions, may have been established at this time by a group related to our archaic matriarchal tradition is found in a Pictish carved stone from a later era that was set at a churchyard in Miegle, Scotland. It depicts an incident in which a mother-goddess-like queen named Vanora, after being kidnapped and forced into infidelity, was sentenced by her husband, the king, to be torn apart and dismembered by wild beasts. The story calls to mind the myth of dismemberment of Sati in the Sakti tradition and of Osiris in the Egyptian tradition. The symbolism of Vanora's name is likely to be found in the Dogon terms *vanu,* which refers to "implementation of the first eight cultivated seeds," and *ra,* which refers to the sun as a symbol of our solar system and of our material universe.

The notion of a queen is one that we associated with the archaic matriarchal tradition in *Point of Origin.* The term implies feminine strength, energy, and mastery and has a linguistic relationship to the concept of an *embrace* that is a signature of that tradition.

As we understand the constructs of the civilizing plan, it seems entirely within the mind-set of the ancestor-teachers to have followed a sensible, symbolic progression when actually establishing regional kingdoms around the world. If, as we surmise, these teachers adopted the Faroe Islands as their safe haven during the era of 3200 BCE, then it also makes sense that they would have made their first attempt at the establishment of a kingship somewhere close to home, where they could easily monitor and manage it. This implies that the teaching center on Orkney Island and regional kingship in Ireland may have been implemented first. It also suggests that the ancestor-teachers chose to follow the symbolic sequence of the progressive stages of matter when fostering these regional kingships, rather than those of agriculture. If so, then Peru would have followed Ireland, then China, and finally Egypt. However, the acknowledged antiquity of the Sphinx suggests that earlier efforts to foster a self-sustaining civilization

Opposite: This carved stone from a churchyard in Miegle, Scotland, depicts Queen Vanora, who, as the result of her infidelity, was sentenced to be dismembered by four lions. © Crown copyright HES.

(apparently based on the same lion symbolism) had been attempted in Egypt. From that perspective, Egypt may have represented the first true attempt, and so it may have constituted the "uncultivated earth" of that earlier effort.

Another outlook on the relative meanings of the terms *aaru* and *taru* is found in the Gaelic language, where the term *eire* implies the geographic direction of west (raising the immediate question, West of what?). The Egyptian phoneme *ar* implies "sunset." Similarly, the Egyptian term *ta* can imply the geographic direction of east and "sunrise." Meanwhile, the Egyptian phoneme *pe* or *per* implies the notion of "sky," a correlate to the concept of the Egyptian term *upper,* indicating the geographic direction of south. An Egyptian term that Budge pronounces as *aaa,* meaning Earth (a counterpart to the Egyptian term *lower,* implying the direction of north), could constitute a correlate to the Chinese *i.* It should be noted that, as with other cosmological references in various cultures, modern directionality is reversed in the Egyptian designations of Upper and Lower. From that outwardly sensible perspective, Aaru would imply the meaning of "Lion of the West," Taru would mean "Lion of the East," Peru "Lion of the South," and Iru "Lion of the North." These interpreted meanings for the terms define the four cardinal directions of an axis and so take on cosmological significance.

Looked at from the perspective of Ireland as a regional kingship and knowing that conceptual terms that carry multiple definitions are a hallmark of the cosmological tradition, we realize that the archaic name for Orkney Island, Argat, could also reasonably be translated as "gateway to Ar (or Eire)." Orkney Island's position to the north of the larger British Isles might lead it to be perceived as a gateway by sea to Scotland, Ireland, or perhaps even Britain. However, Orkney could only be considered a "gateway to Ireland" by someone who happened to approach the island from the north, as compared to some other direction. But based on prevailing ocean currents, anyone who began their journey somewhere south and west of Scotland and used the Atlantic currents to assist them northward would be likely to approach Orkney Island from the north, since the natural flow of the currents might easily bring them to Ireland from that direction.

There has been a lot of historical debate about what the name Orkney means. The early Scandinavian name was Orkneyar or Orknejar. Since aquatic seals are a routine sight near Orkney, the term has been presumed to take its root from the Scandinavian word for "seal," *orkn,* and so would mean Seal Island. (Conversely, similar logic could argue that the seal took its name from the term Orkney.) However, if we interpret the archaic term Argat to mean "gateway to Ar (Eire/Ireland)," then there are several inferences we can potentially make. If we presume that the *ar* in Argat referred to Eire/Ireland, then it's likely that the *ar* in Orkneyar might also refer to Eire/Ireland. From that perspective, we might possibly expect the meaning of the name Orkneyar to also make some coherent statement about Orkney and Eire/Ireland.

Using these criteria as a basis, I searched Budge's *Egyptian Hieroglyphic Dictionary* for a word, or combination of words, that could credibly transliterate to Orkneyar. That search produced the following meaning:

Orkneyar

aar ("to approach")

kheni ("coming by boat")

Ar ("Eire/Ireland")[11]

This interpretation satisfies the phonetic requirements of the name Orkneyar, is consonant with other Faroese/Egyptian word parallels we have proposed, and retains the sense of the archaic term Argat, in that it defines Orkney as a kind of island gatekeeper for Ireland.

17

SESHAT AND THE EGYPTIAN HOUSE OF LIFE

The historical timing of events and evidence from excavated ancient Egyptian artifacts suggest that written language emerged there during the same period as the establishment of dynastic kingship. We have mentioned that an overtly stated tradition in ancient Egypt describes the written hieroglyphic language as having been a gift from their gods, or from our perspective, from the ancestor-teachers. One ongoing focus of the books of this series has been to demonstrate how shapes and concepts of cosmology were seemingly adopted as written glyphs in Egypt, including those represented in stone on Orkney Island.

According to Serge Sauneron in *The Priests of Ancient Egypt,* a tradition of knowledge and instruction similar to what we infer to have existed on Orkney Island was perpetuated as standard features of Egyptian temple complexes, features that he describes as being somewhat mysterious to us. Based on inscribed names that survive as artifacts set in surviving bricks or blocks from the buildings themselves, these included a House of Life and a House of Books, or temple library. Sauneron writes, "These buildings seem to have housed organizations where the sacred knowledge was elaborated and where texts were studied, copied, and collected."[1]

Our understanding of these houses is limited because Egyptian texts speak of them without actually describing them, as if on the assumption that their existence could be taken as common knowledge. A pattern for these houses of instruction was apparently established at Abydos, which was the original seat of government, so they would seem to have been an original feature of the concept of a dynastic temple. Among other duties, it was the job of scribes of these houses to prepare texts for inscription by the artists and masons who built Egyptian temples. Each aspect of sacred knowledge became the domain of priests who made it their specialty. Sauneron says that we know the nature of information held in these libraries because physical examples were preserved and recovered in the town of Tebtunis in Faiyum.[2]

Stephen Quirke states in his book *Ancient Egyptian Religion* that "the House of Life acted as an underpinning of life itself in Egypt."[3] He says that it played an essential role in the annual rituals that reconfirmed royal power at the time of the new year. Those rituals upheld an outlook that kingship in ancient Egypt was postured as a delegated authority. It is clear that this authority was the responsibility of an informed priesthood, comparable to that of the Hogon in Dogon culture, whose job it was to preserve a system of cosmology. It was these "scribes of the house of life" who were masters of both the cosmology and the written hieroglyphic language.

The goddess Seshat, who was associated with the House of Life, is defined by Budge as the goddess of wisdom, learning, and architecture and as the consort of Thoth.[4] George Hart relates in his *Dictionary of Egyptian Gods and Goddesses* that by the time of the Second Dynasty, Seshat was pictured measuring the foundation for a temple, by which we infer that she had responsibility for the ritual alignment of a temple.[5] We know from our studies that this alignment process was understood to replicate the geometry of creation and involved the same sequence of geometric shapes that we see immortalized in stone on Orkney Island.

The name of Seshat rests on the phonetic root *sesh*, which in Egypt defines many of the signature attributes of the mother goddess of our archaic Sakti tradition and so demonstrates conceptual and symbolic links to the archaic tradition. According to Budge, the word *sesh* means "to be white," which in the Sakti and Buddhist traditions is understood to be the color of the deity.[6] It means "to unbolt" or "to draw the bolts of a door,"[7] a cosmological metaphor for the pivoting motion of matter that is most clearly defined in relation to the traditions of ancient China and the Sakti tradition. It also refers to an "arrow," which is an iconic object associated with the Sakti goddesses.

According to Budge, the word *sesh* defines the concept of writing, and it also means "writer, designer, scribe."[8] In addition, the Egyptian word can refer to the concepts of "hair, tress and lock," terms that are symbolized by the spire that tops a Buddhist stupa, the aligned shrine that serves as a grand metaphor for the cosmology. *Sesh* refers to a kind of cake or bread, terms that are treated as cosmological metaphors for mass or matter. The word or phonetic root *sesh* defines the concept of "divisions" and "courses or openings," comparable to the gates between dimensions of the egg of the world that we associate with Ganesha. A brief glance at other Egyptian words that center on the phonetic root *sesh* shows that their meanings encompass many symbols and concepts that are familiar to us from the cosmology.

The Egyptian root *seh* also has significance for the goddess Seshat, tying her conceptually in other ways to important aspects of our archaic tradition. The term refers to a portable Egyptian tent shrine built from poles that were sometimes covered with wooden panels or bound reeds. These shrines were comparable in function to a Siberian yurt. In the Buddhist traditions of Japan, icons that reflected highly secretive cosmological concepts are known to have been deliberately housed in portable shrines as a way of preserving their secrecy through mobility. Early models of the seh shrines were excavated as artifacts at Abydos. These shrines became a prototype for later pharaonic formal architecture.[9]

In some instances, these shrines, which constitute early representations of later temple forms, are built with a hemispheric canopy that sits atop a squared base—the same essential shape (sometimes compared to "handbags") as is reflected on pillars at Gobekli Tepe, where we interpreted them to convey the meaning of "a temple." Barry J. Kemp reports that the tent shrine has been thought to preserve the image of what local temples looked like in the early dynastic period. He says that one actual early shrine was recorded in its completeness at Elephantine in a context that defines it as "a recognizable symbol for shrines and holy places in general."[10]

In similar ways the Dogon phoneme *se* also links us to concepts that are significant cosmologically. The first of these meanings for the term is "clear." Like the Egyptians, aspects of Dogon life and cosmology are expressed in relation to the symbolic notion of a Word. (Genevieve Calame-Griaule, who compiled the *Dictionnaire Dogon,* also authored a book called *Words and the Dogon World.*) Each of eight civilizing skills presented by the ancestor-teachers of the Dogon was counted as a Word. Concepts that define Dogon cosmology fall under the conceptual heading of the Clear Word.[11] Another meaning for the Dogon term *se*—one that would seem to relate directly to the mythical functions of Seshat— is "in good knowledge" or "good harmony." A third meaning, given as "to have, possess, keep for oneself," conjures the image of an embrace that defines the archaic tradition of the mother goddess.[12]

The Sakti tradition celebrated two mother goddesses named Tana Penu and Dharni Penu, who were deemed to have been the "two mothers" of Ganesha and were invariably depicted in his presence. Icons and attributes of these goddesses link them symbolically with the two stars of Sirius, and so by extension to Isis and Nephthys in Egypt. Cyril Aldred tells us in *The Egyptians* that by the time of Pharaoh Menes in the First Dynasty, the king had assumed the title of the Two Ladies, which signified his endorsement by representatives of the goddesses of Upper and Lower Egypt. All of this can be seen to illustrate the perceived transition we believe occurred in this era, from an archaic matriarchal tradition to a more modern one that was primarily patriarchal.

In ancient Egypt, localities could be identified with symbols, much as a seventeenth-century tradesman might place a particular object above his shop door as his trade symbol. These are referred to as "nome signs." The nome sign of Abydos is described by Cyril Aldred as "a beehive-shaped object elevated upon a standard" .[13] However, from our perspective, the figure would be better described as a clay pot (or potbelly) on top of a pillar, both of which were icons of the mother goddess in the Sakti tradition. The Egyptian glyph associated with Seshat can be seen as the combination of the seven-rayed star of the Dogon egg of the world atop a scepter. Similarly, these are figures that associate cosmologically with Ganesha in the Sakti tradition. In the icon, they are surmounted by what we interpret as the shape of a breast (some commentators compare it to an archer's bow), which is symbolic of a mother. In support of this view, Budge defines the word *shesti* to mean "the two breasts," and in our view the symbols of the word define a trailing glyph that is cast as the image of a breast.[14] The combined figure might be interpreted to convey a sense of "the generation or fostering of life," a meaning that fits well with the acknowledged mission of the House of Life in ancient Egypt.

18

VIEWS ON THE PAPAE AND THE PETI

The two cultures known to have been living on Orkney Island in ancient times, identified as the clerical Papae and the pygmy-like Peti, have potential bearing on our outlook on the cosmological history of the region. The era we are most concerned with spans a period of about one thousand years and extends from around 3600 BCE to around 2600 BCE. However, most historical texts that describe the Orkney Island region date from much later periods and were largely written in the early centuries CE or after, at least three millennia later. So far in our discussions, we have outlined several points by which we might favorably compare one of these two groups of ancient inhabitants—the clerics who wore white called the Papae—to the priestly Dogon, or more precisely to predynastic Egyptian ancestors whom we believe to have been contemporaries of the Dogon in the era of 3200 BCE.

Since both the earliest Egyptian pharaohs (if we can judge based on surviving images of pharaohs of the First Dynasty) and the Dogon were clearly descended from black Africans and modern Scandinavians are outwardly Caucasian, the most obvious point to look for as confirmation of our outlook would be any overt reference to the Papae where it is suggested that they may have been of a different race than the Scandinavians. The local tradition in various locales in Northern Scotland such as Caithness is that early inhabitants of the island were black-skinned. One historical text seems to provide us with an initial supporting reference to

115

that effect. Regarding what the early Scandinavian reports say about these ancient inhabitants on Orkney Island, George Barry wrote in *The History of the Orkney Islands*, in 1805:

> On their landing they found, besides their own countrymen, two distinct people, named Peti and Papae, whom they seem to have regarded as different nations.
>
> Many conjectures have been formed respecting both these races of people; who they were; what country they came from; and what was the origin or the etymology of their name.
>
> With regard to the first of them, namely the *Peti,* there is no difficulty whatever; for they are plainly no other than the Peihts, Picts, or Piks; whom, on probable evidence, we have already considered as the aborigines or first inhabitants of this place. And, what puts the matter beyond all doubt, the Scandinavian writers generally call the Piks Peti, or Pets: one of them uses the term Petia, instead of Pictland. . . .
>
> With regard to the *Papae,* it is more difficult to ascertain who they were. Some have thought they were a people that had, in some former age, come from Norway; and in support of this opinion, mention a place of the name of Papafound, in that country. . . .
>
> [One writer] supposes they were the Irish Papas, or priests, who had long been the only clergy in the Pictish dominions; and as they spoke another language, and were also different in their appearance and manners, they might have readily been taken by these strangers for a distinct race, instead of a separate profession.[1]

A thirdhand account given by Herodotus, if we can associate it with Orkney Island based on the geography he cites, is more specific. It tells of a group of men called the Nasamonians, who, attempting to follow the outflow of the Nile River in a westerly direction beyond Libya, were captured and carried off by a group of dwarfish men "under middle height" to a land beyond the Pillars of Hercules (Gibraltar), located near the Celts. Herodotus describes the Celts as dwelling "at the extreme west of Europe," and modern sources show the territory of the Celts to have extended to just across the Strait of Dover eastward from the British Isles. There the group crossed marshy land to a plain with trees and to a town inhabited by men of their own stature who were "black complexioned." The captured men were later able to return safely to their own country. There they described their captors, who were unable to speak the language of the captured men, as "a nation of sorcerers."[2]

If, as we surmise, Orkney Island was created as a ritual training sanctuary, and the Dogon, whom we take as the Papae, were among the initiates trained there, then the strange pygmy-like Peti stand in the conceptual place of the teachers of the Dogon. One title that the Dogon give to their ancestor-teachers is *Nummo*. Symbolically, the Dogon associate their teachers with birds and with water. The Dogon priests suggest that their teachers had an actual physical need to be close to water, and the teachers are described by Marcel Griaule as having deliberately situated themselves near water. Cosmology is closely intertwined with Dogon life, and the term *Nummo* also carries cosmological meanings that relate to water. But because of the dual levels of meaning, it can sometimes be difficult to distinguish which aspects of Dogon lore are purely cosmological and which might also be taken as factual history.

Robert K. G. Temple, in his book *The Sirius Mystery,* makes the seemingly assailable argument that instruction from these mythical teachers constituted an alien contact. We know that both the Dogon and the Buddhists openly assign their "most sacred" knowledge to a nonhuman source and that the Dogon describe this source as having been a spiritual one that was nonphysical or nonmaterial in nature. However, the concerns reportedly expressed by those teachers regarding possible detrimental effects that prolonged contact with them might have on humans imply that there must also have been an actual, physical presence involved, one that would necessarily go beyond mere shamanic insights into some spiritual realm.

Modern researchers are uncertain to whom the term Peti referred, and the consensus opinion is to link them ancestrally to the Picts, an enigmatic and reportedly fierce pygmy tribal group that is known to us from Roman times, some 2,500 years or more after the period of Skara Brae. No one is certain what became of the Peti, and the lack of physical remains on which to base an opinion leads to the supposition that they, like the Picts of more recent historical times, cremated their dead and buried them in mass graves.

Beyond their presumed relationship with the ancient Picts of Scotland, a sensible first step toward inferring the possible identity of the Peti would be to again look to related Egyptian words. Budge gives the Egyptian word Peti as the name of a god. The glyphs of the word read "space" ▢ "and earth/matter" ◠ "together" //, a meaning that would seem to define the fundamental nature of Dogon contact with their teachers. The word is based on the phonetic root *pet,* which implies the simple question "what?"[3] This is the same question that an initiate of the Dogon esoteric tradition is required to continue asking of an informed teacher. From the perspective of the archaic Sakti tradition, through which we trace our instructed cosmology, the word *peti* could be described in relation to the terms "reveal" or "revelation."

In that context, it is extremely interesting that Budge defines an Egyptian word for "pygmy" that he pronounces *nem.*[4] The symbols of one spelling for the word can be interpreted to mean "transmitted" ⌁ "knowledge" 🦅 "spoken" 𓀁. Another spelling is given simply with a single glyph that is the image of a pygmy. It is also suggestive that the Faroese word *nema* means "to learn" and that the Icelandic term for "student" is *nemandi.* Budge lists a second Egyptian word, *nemma,* that he defines as "a man-hawk god, a form of Menu" and whose glyphs define the same pygmy glyph. Budge's definition calls to mind the image of an enigmatic sculpted hawk-like deity that was found at Gobekli Tepe, which would associate the term with our archaic matriarchal tradition. This sculpted image, whose style of dress a hunter-gatherer of the era might not have had a worldview to simply imagine, gives Budge's definition a tangible form and the birds-of-prey symbolism of our archaic tradition a physical rationale. The positioning of the hands of the sculpted hawk god call to mind the amorphous arms and hands that wrap around the end of the Gobekli Tepe pillars, as if in an embrace.

As noted in chapter 13, yet a third word from Budge that is based on the phonetic root *nem*, given as *nemai*, means "island"[5] and so defines the very locale in which we now place the Nemma/Peti. The

Hawk-man figure from Gobekli Tepe,
reputed to be the world's oldest statue. Photo: Jennifur cc by-sa 2.0.

persistent implication is that the ancient group of strange-mannered, sorcerer-like pygmies that were reported to have comported with the Dogon-like clerics on Orkney Island could actually have been the mythical Nummo teachers of the Dogon tradition.

As an added note, the phonetic root *pet* that is part of the name Peti is also rendered as the Egyptian name for Ptah, who rose to prominence during the later patriarchal era of dynastic Egypt, just following the era of Skara Brae. Glyphs of his name read "space" □ "and earth/matter" ⌒ "deified" ⳨ and so also convey the notion of contact between representatives of the nonmaterial and material universes. Ptah is traditionally considered to be a god of creation, the arts, and fertility, all roles that would be entirely appropriate to the Peti if we were to equate them to the Nummo teachers of the Dogon.

One Egyptian term for "sorcerer," defined as a person who speaks "words of power," is *Hekai*. Symbolically, the word reads "the embrace between universes" ⧂ "comes into" 𓅓 "existence" 𓏲𓏲, followed by the spoken-word glyph 𓀁.[6] Budge says that these Hekai were associated with the Tuat, or Underworld, an Egyptian counterpart to the Dogon Second World of matter, whose stages we propose are symbolized by the megalithic structures on Orkney Island. By comparison, the Faroese word *hekti* means "to clasp" or "to embrace."[7]

The problem of positively identifying who the Peti may have been is complicated by our lack of direct knowledge about the Picts. The Picts themselves left no written texts, although they are referred to in the early centuries CE in ancient Roman texts. The term Picti was first mentioned in a Latin poem written in 297 CE.[8] One scholarly viewpoint on the Picts suggests that they have been the object of widespread misperception, carried down in myth and ancient lore.

Accounts of early Roman encounters with the Picts characterize them as an aggressive Celtic tribe that likely migrated across the water to Scotland sometime prior to the rise of the Roman Empire. If so, then they may not have represented the same cultural group as the more archaic Peti. However, attributes that were assigned in very early times to the Peti survived in later times as quasi-mythical traits of the Picts. For example, tradition holds that the Picts—like the Peti—were little people. Anna Ritchie states that "an anonymous Norwegian historian wrote: 'The Picts were little more than pygmies in stature.'"[9] However, later archaeological studies have demonstrated that the Picts were not short of stature but actually of comparable height to other cultures in the British Isles. Again, this argues that the Picts may possibly have been a distinct group from the Peti.

To the extent that we choose to identify the Peti with the Nummo teachers of the Dogon, their tradition holds that after a time, the Nummo teachers may have been forced to leave or chose to leave, either of which could explain the disappearance of the Peti. This transition is considered by the Dogon priests to be a turning point for humanity, one in which the Dogon lost the ongoing support of a knowledgeable, guiding hand.

19
WORDS OF THE SCOTTISH-GAELIC LANGUAGE

If our outlook is a correct one—that Northern Scotland may have been influenced by the same system of cosmology as the Dogon and the Egyptians in ancient times—then it would be reasonable to think that we might find evidence of that system reflected in the Scottish-Gaelic language. There are three linguistically distinct versions of the Gaelic language, known as Irish Gaelic, Manx Gaelic, and Scottish-Gaelic. Although the foundations of these languages are similar, their differences in outward presentation might be compared to those of Spanish and Portuguese. These languages fall under the linguistic classification of a Celtic language, and Scottish-Gaelic has been traditionally thought to have been brought to Scotland, perhaps in the fourth century CE, along with settlers from Ireland. The more recent archaeological outlook is that there is no clear excavated evidence of migrations into or invasions of Scotland that would support that view, so origins for the language remain unclear.[1]

Meanings presented here for Scottish-Gaelic words are taken from Alexander MacBain's *Etymological Dictionary of Scottish-Gaelic*, published in the early 1900s. In the introduction to the dictionary, the author cites broad similarities that are known to exist among languages across Europe and Asia, which he traces historically to regions in southern Russia. Ultimately, he links these to the Aryan language (alternately called Indo-European, Indo-Germanic, or

Indo-Celtic) and dates their earliest usage to at least 3000 BCE.[2]

On Orkney Island, the symbolism we have been pursuing centers on stages in the formation of matter and leads to Skara Brae itself, the village that we think embodies the seven wrapped-up dimensions of the Dogon egg of the world. From there, the trail of symbolism moves on to the agricultural Field of Arou or (in Egyptian terms) Sekhet Aaru. So a likely place to start our discussion of Scottish-Gaelic words would be with the Gaelic word *ar,* which means "plough" or "ploughed land."[3] We interpret the series of megalithic sites on Orkney Island to represent stages of creation, which in our ancient traditions are often characterized as gates. So if we were to consider the archaic name of Orkney Island, Argat, in relation to the meaning of this root, we might interpret it in this context to mean "gateway to the agricultural field."

The cosmological structure that immediately precedes this agricultural field is the Dogon egg of the world, symbolized by the village of Skara Brae. Because the "egg" is described as a bundle of seven wrapped-up dimensions, it is often characterized by the number seven. Appropriately, Alexander MacBain's *Etymological Dictionary of Scottish-Gaelic* gives the word for "seven" as *seachd.*[4] The phonetically similar Egyptian word *skhet* can also refer to a hut built from twigs and branches, comparable to the Jewish sukkah that is built each year to celebrate the seven-day holiday of Sukkhot. (In the Kabbalist tradition of Judaism, the sequence of High Holy Days that includes Sukkhot is understood to symbolize stages of cosmological creation.) The Gaelic word *seachd* is founded on the phonetic root *seac,* which means "to wither" (referring to stalks of corn) and so also relates directly to concepts of agriculture.

We know that the Dogon egg of the world is called the po pilu and is characterized as a spiraling vortex that turns or spins. In chapter 5, we discussed the spinning elephant-headed Indian god Ganesha's relationship to the po pilu, as well as the Tamil word *pil* and the Turkish word *fil,* both of which mean "elephant." So it makes sense that in the Gaelic language, the word *pill* means "turn" and also relates to a root, *till,* that means "turn," "turn round," or "revolve."[5] In his dictionary entry, MacBain adds a note that the word corresponds to the Irish word *pillim,* or *fillim.*

The interchangeable *p* and *f* sounds that we find in archaic words like *pil* and *fil* rest on complex phonetic values that can be substituted for one another. Examples of these are found in the Hebrew language, where we said a set of seven such paired phonemes are applied according to a set of well-understood rules. Our outlook is that some of these archaic terms survived with one pronunciation in some cultures and under the alternate pronunciation in others. It seems clear from this example that similarly interchangeable phonetic pairings also survived in the Irish language.

Within the processes of matter as the Dogon priests describe them, the egg of the world represents the point at which a perceived wave becomes differentiated into discrete units, described by the Dogon as chambers. It is this initial differentiation of matter that we feel is symbolized by the cluster of structures at Skara Brae. Appropriately, the phonetically similar Gaelic word *sgar* means "to separate" or "to sever." MacBain tells us that the related Irish term is *scaraim,* which also means "to separate."[6] Yet another phonetically related Gaelic word, *saoghal,* means "the world" and so repeats the Dogon characterization of their term egg of the world. In much the same way that the terms of Dogon cosmology carry alternate meanings that relate to biological creation, the Gaelic word *saoghal* can also mean "life."[7]

In the Dogon and Egyptian outlooks on the nature of the material world, creation begins in the form of primordial waves and is referred to by the term *nu,* or *nun.* An associated Egyptian goddess of the primeval waters was also known as Nun. Matter is described as ascending in stages from waves, so we associate matter in its wavelike state conceptually with the bottommost levels of creation. Likewise, within the context of the ancient scheme of cosmology we interpret the term *above* to refer to the realm of the macrocosmic universe and the term *below* to relate to the microcosm, where matter emerges. From this perspective, it seems understandable that the Gaelic word *nuas* means "down" or "from above."[8] As the processes of matter ascend upward, they culminate in an atom-like "seed" or "germ" of matter the Dogon call the po. The comparable Egyptian term for "mass, matter or substance" is given by Budge as *pau-t* and relates to an Egyptian god of creation whose name was Pau. These definitions seem consistent with a Scottish-Gaelic word *por,* which means "seed," "spore," or "germ."[9]

One of the signature elements of the Dogon, Buddhist, and Egyptian cosmological systems is found in the unit of measure called the cubit. One Egyptian word for "cubit" is *meh.* It seems likely that this phonetic value forms the root of the modern word *measure.* MacBain defines the phonetically similar Scottish-Gaelic words *me* and *met* to mean "measure."[10] The Egyptian term *maat* referred to an ancient standard of justice and truth by which choices in dynastic Egypt were often judged. It seems possible that this Egyptian concept relates to the Scottish-Gaelic term *maith,* or *math,* meaning "good."[11]

Our outlook that the term Elysian Field may be related to Orkney Island as an instructional sanctuary is supported by the phonetically similar Gaelic words *eilean,* meaning "island," and *eildeir,* meaning "elder." A word with the same pronunciation *eilean* means "training," and the word *eol* means "knowledge."[12] This interpretation is further supported by the phonetically related Gaelic words *eilear,* meaning "a sequestered region," and *eilgheadh,* which refers to the "levelling of a field for sowing" or "first ploughing."[13] So within this single phonetic value *eil/eol,* which takes the same root *el* as the Yahweh-like deity and is a reasonable root for the terms Elysian and the Bay of Skaill, we find expression of the concepts of islands, elders, sequestering, agriculture, and instruction. These meanings encompass virtually all of the key attributes we assign to Orkney Island.

20

THE DRUIDS
AND OTHER PIECES
OF THE PUZZLE

As enigmatic as the early inhabitants of Orkney Island may have been and as sparse as the evidence that can be applied to that puzzle might be, the question of what ultimately became of those same inhabitants seems equally obscure. The traditional archaeological view is that Skara Brae was occupied for approximately six hundred years, beginning at around 3200 BCE and continuing until about 2600 BCE. Within one hundred years or so, that date range coincides with the period that begins the dynastic period in Egypt and extends to the end of Old Kingdom.

Bone evidence suggests that the period of habitation at the village of Skara Brae ended with a grand feast at the nearby Ness of Brodgar, presumably made possible by the stock of domesticated animals that had long been tended there. A specific detail of the feast that intrigues modern archaeologists who have analyzed the pile of bones that was deliberately arranged to surround the site of the feast is that the celebrants left behind only the shinbones of animals.[1] Referring to structures at the Ness of Brodgar, a 2014 *National Geographic* article states:

> Whatever the reason, the ancient temple was decommissioned and partially destroyed, deliberately and symbolically. Before the people moved on, they left behind one final startling surprise for

archeologists to find: the remains of a gargantuan farewell feast. More than 400 cattle were slaughtered, enough meat to have fed thousands of people.

"The bones all appear to have come from a single event," says Ingrid Mainland, an archeo-zoologist from the University of the Highlands and Islands who specializes in ancient livestock. She has been analyzing the piles of bones that were deliberately arranged around the temple. Curiously, the people who ate that final feast left behind only the shinbones of the animals they slaughtered. "What the significance of the tibia was to them, where that fits in the story, is a mystery," says Mainland.[2]

Once again, if we presume a relationship to ancient Egyptian symbolism, it makes sense to examine ancient Egyptian words for clues as to the meaning of the apparent shinbone symbol. One Egyptian term for "shin bones," *setcheb,* is based on the root *s-tcha,* meaning "to go, to depart." A similar word *setcheb* means "disaster, misfortune, calamity."[3] The *National Geographic* article goes on to report, "Next they draped unbutchered deer carcasses over the piles, presumably as offerings. In the center of the chamber they deposited a cattle skull and a large stone engraved with a sort of cup motif."[4]

Again, turning to the Egyptian language for possible insights into the symbolic placing of deer carcasses, we find that the Egyptian word for "deer" was *seshau.*[5] The word is based on the phonetic root *sesha,* which means "to go." Likewise, it calls to mind the name of the Egyptian goddess Seshat, who presided over the next conceptual stage of the civilizing plan, which we see as the emerging agriculturally based kingship at Abydos. Similarly, the reference to the ritually placed cattle head brings us to the Egyptian word *aru,* meaning "cattle for sacrifice."[6] Our ability to link this final ritual act to the same phonetic value as the name that we assign to Orkney Island (Aaru), symbolically affirms the name.

It also seems clear that the stone with the "cup motif" that was uncovered at the center of the Brodgar excavation is carved with a figure that is both familiar and pertinent to our cosmological studies. The "cup" is a match for the Dogon egg in a ball or Egyptian sun glyph figure, the same figure we find among the carvings at Gobekli Tepe. This is the figure we take as a symbol for our material universe, the shape that initiates the processes of creation in the cosmology we have been pursuing. It also arguably became a defining symbol for ancient Egypt.

Shortly after the celebration of the grand feast at the Ness of Brodgar, the village of Skara Brae was covered over—some researchers say by natural forces, others believe (as at Gobekli Tepe and the Ness of Brodgar) as the result of deliberate, careful burial.

To our way of thinking, there are only a few credible motives for the deliberate burial of a sanctuary site, which the Brodgar researchers interpret as a ritual act. One would be to protect it from some foreseeable, impending destruction, as has been argued for the carved megaliths at Gobekli Tepe. However, at Skara Brae, we see that it is not the series of megalithic stone sites that were buried, but rather the somewhat humble (by comparison) and mundane (by Dogon standards) agricultural village and feast sites. Another conceivable motive would be to hide the site from some unknown, adversarial third party. Again if that were the case, why bother to bury the village and feast site but leave standing the series of megalithic stone sites that ultimately lead by road straight to the village?

Yet another possible motive for burial would be to preserve the site during a prolonged absence, assuming the intention was to eventually return and restore it to use. At Skara Brae, the instructional purpose we interpret for the site had been brought to completion. The choice to slaughter and eat the domesticated animals implies that there was an active plan in effect to flatly abandon the site, at least in regard to its presumed instructional purposes.

Another (and in our minds more likely) possibility is that, as the Brodgar researchers conclude, there may have been a ritual motive for so carefully covering over these sites. If so, our experience suggests that we might see that motive reflected in Egyptian words that relate to the

"Cup motif" stone from Ness of Brodgar excavation.
Photo by Isaac Scranton.

processes of burial and "covering over." Budge lists an Egyptian word *arq,* meaning "to tie, to wrap up, to cover over."[7] Symbolically, the word depicts a scroll being tied—the same ritual act that occurs in daily services in Judaism when a Torah scroll, its daily portion having been dutifully read, is carefully tied and placed back in its place of safe storage, in a cabinet that is called an Aron Hakodesh, a term that is often phonetically abbreviated to Ark.

If the choices to kill the remaining livestock and then bury the Skara Brae village site reflect the mind-set of a group that intended to permanently leave Orkney Island, then the suggestion is that, with functioning agricultural kingships established at the four corners of the globe, the Orkney Island site could now be effectively retired. With regard to the former caretakers of Orkney Island—the Peti and the Papae—it seems clear that many of the Papae, who may have been black Africans, may have become the earliest kings, pharaohs, and priests of Egypt, China, Ireland, and perhaps Peru. Surviving images of First Dynasty pharaohs in Egypt give the distinct impression that they were genetically black African. The priestly Na-Khi from the borderland between Tibet and China are traditionally understood to have been black, and in that region, the term *na* actually took on the meaning of "black." As we stated in chapter 3, DNA studies in Scotland have shown both Tuareg and Berber (predynastic Egyptian) genetic influences, which are comparable to those found in the Dogon, who are black African.

At this point, we infer that Orkney Island took on its role as the Elysian Fields, a quasi-mythical land of the dead. As such, the covering over of the village may have served as a kind of demonstrational burial ritual, symbolic of death rituals that would be appropriate for a person. Budge lists an Egyptian word *Tuat* that he defines as meaning "a very ancient name for the land of the dead."[8] Symbolically, it reads "the giving" ⬭ "of agriculture" 𓊽 "and matters" ⌒ "civic" ⊗. From that perspective, careful burial may imply the notion of successful completion of purpose. Budge defines another word, *tua-t,* to mean "plant," but the glyphs of the word suggest that the term referred to "matters agricultural."[9] The Tuatiu were the "gods and other beings of the Tuat,"[10] while the phonetic root *tua* means "to bear, to carry, to support."

We have argued that the phonetic root *ar* underlies the Dogon and Egyptian terms *arou* and *aaru* and links Dogon cosmology to the Egyptian concept of the Elysian Fields. It is evident in the Dogon term *arq,* which is a name for the stupa-like aligned ritual granary shrine that evokes stages of creation comparable to the megalithic sites on Orkney Island. We see it again in the ancient names Argat and Orkneyar. Aaru, or Lion of the West, is the term we believe was assigned to Ireland at the time of the establishment of the four regional kingships at around 3100 BCE, a geographic counterpart to Egypt as Taru, or Lion of the East. So it seems likely that the term *ar* constitutes the phonetic root of the ancient name for Ireland, Eire.

There are good reasons to think that when ongoing instruction at Orkney Island came to a close, the Nummo/Nem/Peti (or their closest followers) chose to move on to nearby locales, including Ireland. By around 1800 BCE, some sources acknowledge the presence in Ireland of a group called the Tuatha Danaan (sometimes given as Tuatha de Danaan). This was a tribe devoted to the goddess Dana. It is interesting to note that the form of the name of the tribe, formulated to express the name of the deity they celebrated, follows the same essential tribal naming convention we have observed in connection with the cosmology we have been pursuing. The name Dana calls to mind the earth goddess of the Sakti cult, Tana Penu. In ancient Greece, Diana was a goddess of the hunt, and we know that the arrow was an archaic icon of Tana Penu in India. In Egypt, at this time of apparent transition from an archaic matriarchal system to one that was patriarchal, there was also a "very ancient Earth-God" Tanen and his consort Tanen-t.[11] Another Egyptian word *tua* means "supporter" or "adherent."[12] So the combined name Tuatha Danaan, interpreted in relation to Egyptian roots, makes sense as "supporters of Tanen/Tanen-t."

The Scottish-Gaelic word *tan* means "time."[13] In our outlook on ancient cosmology, the existence of the dimension of time in the material universe is the factor that differentiates it from its nonmaterial paired twin. Time is the fourth dimension that ultimately defines ours as the fourth of seven universe stages. Looked at from the phonetic perspective of an originally oral cosmological tradition, *ta* implies the concept of earth or mass. We understand the goddess name Tana to combine the phoneme *ta* (earth) with the phoneme *na* (mother) to produce the name of the Sakti earth mother goddess.

Budge notes that there was also a mythical Egyptian locality called Tanen-t that was an "important sanctuary of Seker." The Egyptian word *seker* means "to inform" and also refers to "celestial existence" or concepts of creation."[14] We have already noted that the Egyptian term *sekhet,* as used in the term Sekhet Aaru, means "field." So there is a reasonable perspective from which the term *seker* might be seen to refer to Orkney Island.

One nineteenth-century view was that the Tuatha Danaan had migrated to Ireland from Scythia, which is a region of the Fertile Crescent that coincides with the locale of Gobekli Tepe. They were descended from Nemed, the leader of a group called the Muintir Nemed (or Muintir Neimhidh), or people of Nemed. The group is sometimes referred to as the Clann Nemid, or offspring of Nemed. We may recall that *nem* was the Egyptian term for "pygmy," which we associate with both the Peti and the Nummo teachers of the Dogon. The Tuatha Danaan were also predecessors to the Druids, who later took up residence in Scotland, Ireland, and France.

We also recall that the abducted sailors from Herodotus's tale described their pygmy abductors as "sorcerers." So it is interesting that the Scottish-Gaelic word *druidh* means "a magician."[15] According to MacBain, it relates to the word *draoi,* whose etymology is obscure; it means "magician, druid," but it can also mean "agriculturist."[16] Both meanings would seem to uphold a likely connection between those who were on Orkney Island in ancient times and the later Druids.

It is generally understood that all Druid populations, without regard to specific region, practiced the same religion.[17] Like Dogon cosmology, Druid teachings represented a closely held body of secret knowledge that centered on natural laws. As we interpret the references, it was also understood in ancient Egypt that the notion of a deity rested on concepts of natural law. In describing the nature of that religion, John Healy writes in *Insula Sanctorum et Doctorum; or Ireland's Ancient Schools and Scholars,* "Their learning, at least in Gaul, consisted for the most part in rather fanciful theories about the heavenly bodies, the laws of nature, and the attributes of the pagan deities. These doctrines, like their religious tenets, were not committed to writing but were handed down by oral tradition; for they wished above all things to keep their knowledge to themselves, and to impress the common people with a mysterious awe for their own power and wisdom. It has been said by some writers that Druidism was a philosophy rather than a religion."[18]

In Dogon culture, an initiate requires a lengthy period of inquiry, often extending to decades, in order to attain the innermost secrets of the tradition. Marcel Griaule attained his initiated status among the Dogon during his third decade of intermittent anthropological study. Ancient Greek references suggest that some of Greece's greatest classical minds studied with Egyptian priests for twenty or more years so as to acquire Egyptian knowledge. Similarly, Healy writes of the Druids, "A . . . long course of instruction, generally extending to twenty years, was required for their disciples."[19]

Much as the Dogon have a top-ranking priest known as the Priest of Arou and Judaism preserves the tradition of a high priest, the Druids had an arch-Druid who was elected for life. It seems reasonable that the title *arch* may have derived from the same term *ark* that the Dogon apply to their aligned shrine and that is found in the Egyptian term *arq-hehtt*.

As with Dogon cosmology, Healy tells us that Druid knowledge was also an oral tradition. The notion that Druid knowledge was linked to Dogon-like civilizing skills is reflected in an alternate designation for the Tuatha Danaan, given by some early Irish authors as Tri de Dana. This term is translated to mean "three gods of craftsmanship." Again like the Dogon, the tribe differentiated three gods whose definition related to learned skills but did not actually worship them.

One commonality that would seem to link the Dogon in Africa, the Papae on Orkney Island, and the Druids in Ireland is the wearing of signature tunics by all three groups. Genevieve Calame-Griaule defines the tunic as a traditional Dogon item of apparel and defines a number of traditional types, each delineated with its own distinct designation. The generic term for a tunic is *aru goy* or *argoy*.[20] We understand that term *aru* serves to associate the garment with both the Dogon Priest of Arou and the Field of Arou and so relates conceptually to our view of Orkney Island. The term *goy,* as used in colloquial Judaism, we take as a reference to the common populace. This implication (confirmed by Calame-Griaule) is that this is the traditional garb of the people.

The similarities of garb between the Celtic Druid priests and the modern-day Hogon of Dogon society began with the often bare-legged clerics wearing the same style of tunic as protective outerwear over a long white shirt. Likewise, the hat of the Druid could well fit the style of floppy hat often worn by the Dogon priest or diviner. In a further resemblance, each typically carried a long wooden staff which could be employed either as a walking stick or as a writing implement to trace drawings in the sand.

Modern artistic renderings of written descriptions of Celtic Druid priests, such as those by artist Erica Guilane-Nachez, have direct comparability to the traditional garb of a modern-day Hogon, as evident in images such as those from the *National Geographic* photograph series of the Dogon of Southern Mali, West Africa, by Chris Rainier.

Budge gives one Egyptian word for "tunic" as *aaa,*[21] the same phonetic value we associate with the name of the Hebrew god Yah. Symbolically, the word reads "embrace" ⸻ ⸻ "comes to be" 🐦 . From our perspective, both of these concepts (that of the embrace given in relation to two arms and the deity Yah) associate with the sanctuary at Gobekli Tepe. The name of the god El (whom we take as a counterpart to Yah) associates with the sanctuary on Orkney Island.

Another Egyptian word for "tunic" is *het,*[22] the same term that we associate with the concept of a temple. On one level, the archaic notion of a temple is conceptualized as an embrace between the non-material and material universes. Since these universes relate symbolically to the geometric figures of a circle and a square, respectively, the circular/squared figure of a hemisphere or dome comes to represent the concept of the embrace. Symbolically, the word *het* reads "universal" ⦿ "embrace" ⌓, followed by the looped string glyph ⬡. Consonant with this Egyptian word, the Faroese word *hetta* means "hood," suggestive of a hooded tunic.[23] Appropriate to our interpretation, Parker includes the meaning of "dome" as a synonym for the word.

Budge gives yet another Egyptian word for "tunic" as *sat.*[24] This pronunciation links us to the mother goddess Sati of the Sakti tradition. Symbolically, the word reads "another" ∥ "coming" (read "example") 🐦 "of the dome/embrace" ⌓. Still another Egyptian word for "tunic" is *suar.*[25] This word forms the phonetic root of the word *s-uarekh,* meaning "to make green or fertile," and so connects us to the concepts of instructed agriculture that we associate with Orkney Island.

A similar tradition of wearing tunics is preserved in modern Judaism in the form of the *Talit Katan* (sometimes referred to with the generic term *ketonet*), a kind of tunic that is worn by priests under their clothes when they served in the tabernacle or the temple in Jerusalem.

21

The Hindu Parable of the Seven Houses

In the mindset of the ancient cosmology, one metaphor that recurs in various cultures is the characterization of the nonmaterial universe as a sleeping goddess, and the processes of creation in the material universe (the Egyptian Underworld and Dogon Second World of matter) as an awakening. In the case of Skara Brae, it is the architecture of a house that takes the specific form of a sleeping woman (based on the cosmological metaphors, we might infer her to be a sleeping goddess) that provides critical linkage to Dogon and Egyptian architecture, language, cosmology, and symbolism as essential keys for interpreting the poorly understood symbolic elements we encounter on Orkney Island. These keys lead us to interpret Orkney Island as a real-world geographic locale, linked to pivotal concepts of death and the Underworld in ancient Egypt and ancient Greece. Knowing this, it behooves us to explore the mythic foundations that may relate to mother goddesses, houses, deceased spirits, and the Underworld in the traditions we have studied previously, most particularly those of ancient India and Egypt.

In our discussions of possible meanings of the word *pharaoh* and its Egyptian correlate *per-aa,* we proposed in chapter 13 a likely phonetic link to the Hindu Purana texts. Our outlook is that the word *puran* is formed from the roots *per,* meaning "structure," and *an,* which means "offering," and, like the Orkney Island structures, implies progressive stages of creation. One particular Purana text is the Devi Puran, whose focus is on the nature and attributes of an ancient mother goddess of the Sakti tradition named Devi. Like other surrogate goddesses in India, Devi was looked on as the divine world mother, was understood to represent both a biological mother and the mother earth, and was symbolic of the feminine energy of the nonmaterial universe.

Of particular interest to us is a popular fable that is repeated by Janaky Sharma in her book *Devi Puran.* It tells of how the goddess Devi sets out on a journey at dusk to visit seven homes. The storyline of the fable relates what she finds when she arrives at each home, characterized by a particular action that was being undertaken by the housewife who lived within it.[1] As we might expect from any cosmological reference that is given in relation to seven or eight houses or chambers, and even without regard to the story's classification in this case as a Puran, our reasonable guess would be that the fable outlines stages of creation. In this case, it seems to have been specifically cast to represent seven progressive stages in the formation of matter.

When approaching ancient mythical storylines, it is important to consider that the cosmology we are pursuing was originally an oral tradition, meaning that the meanings of terms often rested on how they were pronounced. As we understand the system to have worked, each term carried two or more discrete meanings that were pronounced the same way, so in any given case the intended meaning rested on context, much as the modern listener of spoken English interprets the meaning of *their* from *there* or *they're.* When symbolic written language, such as the Egyptian hieroglyphic language, was adopted, these phonetically similar words might have been conveyed by different glyphs, since the spelling of a specific word seems to have been dictated by its conceptual meaning. As a consequence, these grouped meanings play out in the Egyptian hieroglyphic language as homonyms of one another—words that are pronounced similarly but spelled differently.

Our experience with symbolic references as they appear in ancient cosmological myths is that homonyms were often used to disguise meaning. In *China's Cosmological Prehistory* we cited many examples of myths in which the attributes or actions of a Chinese emperor were conveyed using words that for the Egyptians were homonyms of one another. The suggestion is that one purpose of the story was to record the multiple meanings of a single cosmological term.

Based on this understanding that each cosmological term carries multiple meanings and that those meanings cross the boundaries of culture and language, and knowing that the meanings express themselves as homonyms of one another in the Egyptian hieroglyphic language, we have chosen to interpret the very careful terminology of the Hindu fable by comparing it to words of the Egyptian hieroglyphic language. This choice also seems sensible, since Egyptian glyphs often provide us with valuable symbolic and conceptual insights into the likely intended meaning of any given word.

According to the Hindu fable, when Devi arrives at the first house, she finds the housewife sleeping. Symbolically, an Egyptian word for "sleep" is pronounced *aaa,* phonetically similar to the name of the Hebrew deity Yah. When interpreted conceptually, the word reads "the coming" 🦅 "of the embrace" ⌐ ⌐ "of" // "perception" 👁.[2] From a symbolic perspective, sleeping people reenter the realities of the waking world when they open their eyes and once again start to perceive it. That act of waking up is equated with the initial stirrings of creation after matter in its wavelike form has been perceived. From a cosmological perspective, the glyphs of the Egyptian word imply the notion of an act of perception that brings the nonmaterial, feminine aspect of the universe into contact with the material, male aspect. It is this interface between the nonmaterial and material aspects of the universe that is said to catalyze the processes of creation. We understand that the nature of the nonmaterial, feminine aspect of the universe is akin to light, much as in the material universe the shining of light is what facilitates a person's actual ability to see.

In the Dogon culture, the term *ie,* which is phonetically similar to the Egyptian *aaa* and the Hebrew Yah, means "to view," "to perceive," or "to find what we are looking for."[3] This meaning coincides with the act of perception that, from a scientific perspective, is a catalyst to the transformation of matter in its wavelike state into particles. However, the Dogon designation *ie pilu* is also the term for a month of the lunar calendar, which is used to regulate the agricultural cycle. The term *pilu* overtly associates the concept with the stages of the Dogon egg of the world, which is known as the po pilu. The calendar resets itself at the time of the harvest (in October) and counts forward from there. Many of the Dogon month names bear a relationship to the names of the ordinal numbers, so their progression replicates the act of counting. The month names also often bear a resemblance to cosmological terms, names of deities, and names of astronomic structures in various ancient cultures.

In the second house, the housewife is encountered eating. An Egyptian word for "eat" is *aam,* which is phonetically similar to the name of the Dogon deity Amma. Symbolically, the word reads "that which" ⎮ "gives" ⏝ "knowledge" 𓅆 .[4] Instructed knowledge of agriculture—the civilizing skill that allows a society to feed itself—is what we have proposed was occurring at the Field of Arou on Orkney Island. Instructed knowledge is what the Dogon priests specifically task themselves with preserving, and according to Barry J. Kemp agriculture is the single societal skill that was a prerequisite to the establishment of the earliest civilizations.

In the third house, the housewife is found cutting her nails. Budge gives the Egyptian word for "to cut or pare the nails" as *sesh,* which is phonetically similar to the name of the Egyptian goddess Seshat. Symbolically, the Egyptian word reads "the work" ⚬ "of the island" ⬭ "field" ▦ "is given" ⌣.[5] Again, by our interpretation, the "work of the island field" on Orkney Island at 3200 BCE was agriculture, and we know that dynastic kingship based on agriculture appeared in Egypt around 3100 BCE at Abydos. The mother goddess celebrated at Abydos was Seshat.

Based on these first three sets of meanings, the suggestion is that the steps in which the instructed civilizing plan seems to have been implemented may have been meant to mirror the sequential stages of how matter forms. There is clearly also a perspective from which these events of the fable align with the first three phases of ancient instructed knowledge, as we believe them to have occurred historically. For example, in the case of first house that Devi visits, the notion of an embrace, which is characterized symbolically within the word *sleep* by two arm glyphs ⎯⏌ ⎯⏌, is what we also find enshrined as emergent arms on the carved pillars at Gobekli Tepe, a locale that is widely characterized as "the first temple." The archaic Egyptian name we assign to the temple structure at Gobekli Tepe is Getpetkai, a word that we see as a credible rendering of the modern term Gobekli. When we apply a more modernized pronunciation to the glyphs of the word Getpetkai, we interpret it as Het Pet Ka Yah, meaning "temple of space embracing light"—the same essential meaning that we interpret for the Egyptian word for "sleep." Likewise, we know that in the book of Genesis, the first documented act of the Hebrew god Yah, while hovering over the face of the waters, is to essentially turn night into day, comparable to what a person experiences as he or she wakes up.

The second house relates to the name of the Dogon creator god Amma and to the concept of instructed knowledge. From our perspective, the sanctuary we believe existed on Orkney Island relates to the Dogon and the Nummo teachers who ostensibly provided them with instructed knowledge. The outward parallelism of the sequence of houses, the sequence of instructional sanctuaries, and the related deities suggests a pattern.

The third house relates to the goddess Seshat and to the notion of island-related agricultural instruction having been given. These are both concepts that directly pertain to the establishment of dynastic kingship at Abydos, where Seshat was celebrated. So again, the case of the third house can be seen to uphold our progression of perceived parallels. This perspective on possible stages of instructed knowledge and their apparent symbolism provides us with a rationale by which to understand the seemingly abrupt appearance of Seshat at Abydos, hand in hand with dynastic kingship. We can see that her name, like those of Yah and Amma, seems to be symbolic of the stage of implementation of the civilizing plan that is represented there.

The Hindu fable of Devi's visits continues through the remainder of the seven houses in similar fashion. For example, in the fourth house, the housewife is found fighting. Egyptian words for "fight" are given in relation to the phonetic root *aab,* which is associated with Egyptian words for elephants, tusks, and numerous other meanings that are attributes of the Vedic god Ganesha.[6] In India, Ganesha is known as the gatekeeper and so symbolizes the "gates" between the seven wrapped dimensions of the egg of the world that appear to be symbolized by the houses of the Hindu fable.

The housewife in the fifth house is found sweeping the house. An Egyptian word for "to sweep out" is *sesher,* which again coincides with the Egyptian goddess Seshat. However, in this case, the word is most closely pronounced like a term that means "to emit light"[7] and so now likely relates to the formation and first appearance of light within the material universe, as opposed to the intermingling of the nonmaterial energy with the material essence that is indicated at the first house.

At the sixth home, the housewife is picking lice from someone's head. The Egyptian term for "louse" or "lice" is *pai.*[8] It is formed on the phonetic root *pa,* which is the cosmological term for "mass" or "matter." Appropriate to that interpretation, according to Budge, Pau was a primeval god whose name meant "he who exists." The Egyptian word *pau-t* means "stuff, matter or substance."[9]

At the seventh home, the housewife is said to be very poor and humble, but also very spiritual, and so she is found praying. An Egyptian word for "pray" is *pteh,* which is the name of the Egyptian god Pteh, or Ptah.[10] Within the cosmology, *pet* is a term we associate with the formation of space. Looked at from the standpoint of an astrophysicist, the fable seems to define a progression of creation for the material universe in which light forms, then mass, then space.

When Devi comes upon the woman in the seventh house, her joy knows no bounds, and she ends up lavishing blessings on the woman. One Egyptian term for "joy" is *aut ab,* and it refers to the notion of "the swelling of the heart."[11] The word *heart* is a term that is sometimes applied symbolically to the Dogon egg of the world, the vibrating, chambered structure of matter that swells and, at its eighth conceptual stage, ultimately bursts. The Egyptian term is based on the phonetic root *au,* which means "to make an offering," and so reflects the supplicating acts of the devout woman in the seventh house of the fable.

Several of these same phonetic roots and the conceptual progression they imply are evident in words from Orkney Island. References to the god El (whom we see as a surrogate of the Hebrew god Yah), the phonetic structure of the roots of the word Elysian, and the symbolic emphasis on reeds and the color white (symbolic of light) are consistent with attributes of the god Yah. The presence of Dogon-like teachers and initiates on the island implies a likely connection to the concept of Amma. The names of the Peti and the Papae are based on phonetic roots that could relate to Pteh/Ptah and the Dogon and Egyptian concepts of po and pau. In our view, instruction given on the island resulted in the establishment of dynastic kingship at Abydos (based on the phonetic root *ab*), overseen by a goddess named Seshat (formed from the phonetic root *sesh*).

The fable of Devi's visits to the seven houses can also be understood on another level of interpretation that relates to the instructed civilizing plan. From this perspective, the houses represent *levels of a person's physical needs* that must be satisfied in order for them to succeed within a society. These needs might compare to the items in Abraham Maslow's hierarchy of needs as they are understood in the field of psychology.

From this outlook, the concept of a house itself satisfies what is arguably a person's first basic need—the need for shelter and, as the action of the first housewife suggests, a place to sleep. The second housewife was found eating and so demonstrates what might be a person's next basic need, which is for food. The third housewife is found cutting her nails and so might symbolize the idea of personal maintenance, such as the need to groom and clean oneself.

THE HINDU PARABLE OF THE SEVEN HOUSES   143

The act of the fourth housewife, who is found fighting, underscores yet another basic need of a person, which is for personal safety. In the fifth house, the housewife is found sweeping. This act might symbolize the need to maintain a clean personal environment. At the sixth house, the housewife picks lice from a person's hair. Her act implies the need of an individual to be of service to others. The poor but spiritual woman found in the seventh house suggests a need to place the spiritual aspects of life above material acquisitions.

Like many of the myths we have explored in other traditions, there is a perspective from which the fable of Devi and the seven houses can be seen to encode the multiple meanings of a single cosmological term. In relation to the Egyptian hieroglyphic language, the phonetic root of the term is *neh,* and in accordance with our level-of-needs discussion, various meanings derived from that root center on the concept of personal needs.

The term *need,* the concept on which these meanings are based, is expressed by the Egyptian word *nehet.* We can relate the Egyptian terms to the notion of a Devi-like mother goddess through the name Nehit, which Budge defines as the "mother of the gods in the boat of Ra."[12] That definition suggests a possible origin for the great Egyptian mother goddess Net, or Neith, herself conceptually linked to Devi through language. This link seems sensible when we consider that the Egyptian word *neh-t* means "defense" or "protection"[13] and, based on discussions found in *Point of Origin,* that the Egyptian word *het* can mean "house" or "temple." Through the combined phonetics *neh-het,* these basic life needs are conceptually defined as "protections of the house." One traditional outlook on the Egyptian goddess Neith associates her with the image of crossed arrows and a shield and so aligns her with the concepts of defense and protection. The arrow is also a traditional icon of the mother goddess in the Sakti tradition.

In support of this outlook on the fable, we find that Budge lists an Egyptian word *nehas* that means "to awaken" or "wake up,"[14] which we have said is a metaphor for material creation and reflects events at the first of the houses that Devi visits. (A house satisfies our need for shelter as we sleep.) As we have cited above, the Egyptian word *neh-t* means "defense" or "protection," which relates to the housewife who is found fighting in the fourth house. (The structure of a house protects us from attack.) The Egyptian root *neha* is one that relates to terms of health and medicine, which relate to the housewife's act of removing lice in the sixth house. Budge defines a word *nehar* that specifically means "disease."[15] (The house shelters us, keeps us warm and healthy, and is a place to recover when we're ill.) The Egyptian word *nehu* means "poor" or "destitute"[16]—the condition in which Devi finds the woman in the seventh house—and the word *neh* means "to ask, petition, request, or pray,"[17] consistent with her supplicating demeanor. The archaic Egyptian word for "house," *het,* also means "temple." Furthermore, Budge includes a dictionary entry for the word *neham,*[18] which means "to rejoice" or "cry out in pleasure," which defines Devi's own act in response to finding a devout woman in the seventh house. It also embodies the concept of "celebration," which is the archaic term that stood in the conceptual place of "supplication" or "prayer" in later traditions.

On yet another level, these constructs that relate to Devi can be understood in relation to the Buddhist concept of *ascension,* a word that defines notions of enlightenment and rebirth. *Ascension* is also the term that is applied to the progressive stages through which matter passes. Adrian Snodgrass, the authority on Buddhist symbolism who authored *The Symbolism of the Stupa,* defines a Buddhist concept called *devayana,* which, in all likelihood, the goddess Devi personifies. The term relates to a gateway that gives humanity access to what Snodgrass describes as a "Pathway to the Gods" or alternately as the "Pathway of the Forefathers." He states that this path is traversed by *unregenerate men.* He says of the gate that "it is simultaneously an exit and an entry. The *Comprehensor* . . . ascends to the Northern Gate and passes through, never to return unless to aid and guide those who follow; but the ignorant fall back to the Southern Gate, pass out . . . and are reborn into yet another level of existence"[19] (italics added).

22

THE EGYPTIAN TALE OF THE "SEVEN HOUSES IN THE OTHER WORLD"

Following our discussion of the Hindu parable of the seven houses, it seems significant that there was also a comparable, but more extensive, Egyptian tale of seven houses, included as a section of *The Egyptian Book of the Dead*. Our source reference for the Egyptian tale is a translation by Normandi Ellis, taken from the book *Awakening Osiris: The Egyptian Book of the Dead* in the chapter titled, "Seven Houses in the Other World."[1] The seven houses of the Egyptian tale were explicitly assigned to the Other World or the Underworld, the mythical Egyptian realm that we associate with the Dogon Second World of matter. This is the same cosmological region that we inferred was symbolized in the Hindu parable.

The Hindu story is given in relation to the goddess Devi and describes the series of housewives she encounters within the houses, which from our perspective corresponds thematically to the archaic matriarchal tradition. By contrast, the Egyptian tale is told from the point of view of the spirit of a deceased person, self-described as an old man (sometimes interpreted to be the spirit of a deceased pharaoh), and it focuses on progressive sets of three gods whom the spirit finds waiting just inside the doorway of each house. This emphasis in the Egyptian tale on a male spirit and gods, rather than the Hindu goddess and housewives of the Hindu fable, might be seen as reflective of the patriarchal view of the dynastic era of Egypt.

In the storyline of the Egyptian tale, each of the seven structures is characterized as a *house of challenge* for the deceased person's spirit to traverse. We can interpret the symbolic meaning of the term *challenge* in relation to Budge's dictionary entry for the word, pronounced *ser*.[2] The same word can also mean "arrange" or "order" and so likely refers to an ordered sequence, such as the houses present. The word *ser* calls to mind the Islamic concept of the Bridge of Sirah and the Kabbalist tradition of N'Sirah, or Nisera, which relate to ancient processes of creation. It also suggests the modern root *ser*, meaning "to be," as it is defined in the Spanish language.

From a cosmological perspective, the seven houses most obviously equate to the same seven wrapped-up dimensions of the Dogon egg of the world (defined as eight conceptual stages) that we relate to the Skara Brae houses. We proposed in *Sacred Symbols of the Dogon* that the Egyptian term for these dimensions is *arit*.[3] The phoneme *ar* (as discussed in chapter 10 of the present book) refers to ascending stages of creation. According to Budge, the Egyptian word *ri* means "door" and *rit* means "gate."[4] So the combined term *arit* can be seen as an effective counterpart to the ancient name for Orkney Island, Argat, a term that we believe made reference to its series of megalithic sites, characterized as "gateways." Similarly, an Egyptian term for "friend, associate, companion" was *ari*,[5] which is found as the prefix to several ancient Egyptian terms for "wives." So from a purely phonetic standpoint, the concepts of a "house" and a "housewife" seem like good symbolic masks for the notion of an *arit*, and they might serve as one conceptual link between the Hindu and Egyptian stories.

THE FIRST HOUSE

When the spirit traveler of the Egyptian storyline reaches the first house, he encounters three gods just inside the doorway, who are said to be dreaming. He refers to the first god as a watchman, the second as a doorkeeper, and the third as a herald. These designations (which could apply to the gods of each house) confirm a relationship between the houses and the Egyptian concept of an arit, since in Budge's dictionary entry for the seven arits, he notes that each was also assigned a watcher, a doorkeeper, and a herald.[6] We interpret the term *watcher* to refer to an act of perception associated with light, the term *doorkeeper* to refer to a gateway between the dimensions of the egg of the world, and the term *herald* to refer to the repeating loops of the spiral of the egg. The term *arit* itself relates to a phonetic root *ari,* which also refers to light.

As the Egyptian story continues, the traveler's spirit repeatedly implores the three gods to let him pass. In his initial admonition he somewhat enigmatically cries, "You, doorkeeper, upside-down face!" One Egyptian word for "upside-down" is *skhet,*[7] and Budge cites a word for "face" that is pronounced *her.*[8] Arguably, the spirit has spoken, as his very first direct statement of the tale, words that are the phonetic equivalent of Skhet-Aaru, the name of the Field of Reeds. This term effectively associates the tale with the Second World of matter as the Dogon understand it and the agricultural site on Orkney Island, as well as the locale through which the traveler's spirit journeys in *The Egyptian Book of the Dead.*

The description of the dreaming state of these three gods coincides with that of the housewife who is found sleeping by the goddess Devi in the first house of the Hindu parable. An Egyptian word for "dream," *upsh,* is a homonym for a word that means "to give light."[9] In relation to the Hindu parable, our interpretation is that the first house pertains to the god Yah and represents the initial embrace that introduces the feminine energy of the nonmaterial universe (defined as being like light) to the masculine energy of the material universe and thereby catalyzes the processes of creation, which are in turn characterized as an awakening.

According to the *Egyptian Book of the Dead* tale, the first of the three gods of this initial house has the head of a crocodile, the second holds an ear of corn, and rising up between them stands a third god, who is described as being "as straight as a pillar of stone." When we look to Budge for possible clues to the symbolic meanings of the terms *crocodile, corn,* and *pillar,* we find that words for all three concepts are formed on the phonetic value *at.* We may recall that key words used to define the first house of the Hindu parable led us to the very similar phonetic values *aaa,* Yah, and *ie.*

The spirit entreats the three gods to "let the memory of an old man pass!" According to Budge, the Egyptian word for "memory" is *mau.* However, Budge also interprets Mau as the name of a god of light,[10] so we see repetition of the same light symbolism that relates cosmologically to the Hebrew god Yah. Similarly, the phonetic root *ma* refers to the act of perception that causes matter in its wavelike state to transform into particles. Egyptian words for "old man" center on the phonetic roots *a* and *au.*[11] (The Hebrew word for "light" is similarly pronounced *aur.*) Meanwhile, the notion of "the memory of an old man" would seem like a very good metaphor for the concept of time, and Budge gives an Egyptian word for "time" phonetically (once again) as *at.*[12] Time or duration is the dimensional attribute that is said to differentiate our material universe from its nonmaterial twin. Looked at from a scientific perspective, it seems fair to postulate that the concept of time comes into existence at the first stage of the creation of matter and so is symbolically appropriate to the first house of the Other World.

The spirit repeatedly demands of the gods of the first house to "let me pass." One Egyptian word for "pass," "move on," or "pass by" is *nen.*[13] Budge notes that the same term relates to the passing of years and so supports an interpretation that relates to concepts of time. Budge also tells us that the Neniu (or Nuiu) were "a group of four goddesses who befriended the dead" but are also alternately defined as "beings who observe or keep watch over time, the divine timekeepers in the Tuat." Moreover, the word *nen* can also refer both to the concept of a thread, from which matter is said to be woven, and to a bundle of reeds, the symbol that we think defines the Orkney Island site.

Additionally, Budge tells us that the term *nen-t* refers to "the place where nothing is done," which he takes to be "the grave."[14] However, we also know that the nonmaterial universe is defined in the archaic traditions of India as having perfect knowledge, but with an inability to act, presumably due to the lack of duration of time. The suggestion is that, just as the term *nun* refers cosmologically to matter in its wavelike state, the term *nen* may refer to its nonmaterial aspect, which is said to exist outside the confines of space and time.

Descriptions within the Egyptian tale associate the first house (representative of the first stage of creation) with the image of a tall pillar. This is the same symbolism we assign to the standing pillar of the Watchstone of Stenness and to the single reedleaf glyph 𓏤 in the ancient Egyptian hieroglyphic language. Likewise, the symbolism applies to the central gnomon of the base plan of a Buddhist stupa. The tall pillar of the tale is also a conceptual correlate to the Gobekli Tepe pillar that we interpret as being embraced by its two carved arms. Our outlook is that this pillar represents the concept of "that which is" or the notion of "coming into being"—the very first stage of creation.

Another admonition the spirit makes to the doorkeeper of the first house is to cry out, "You creature of many forms!" An Egyptian word for "creature" is *ari-t*[15]—the very same Egyptian term we associate cosmologically with the seven houses. Budge lists two terms for "many formed." The first he gives as *aa aru*,[16] or as we interpret it phonetically, "light of Arou." The second he pronounces *kheperu*,[17] the name of the Egyptian dung beetle that, from our perspective, represents the notion of nonexistence coming into existence.

THE SECOND HOUSE

As the deceased spirit enters the second house, he encounters three gods who are said to be conspiring. An Egyptian word that means "to conspire against" is pronounced *negemgem*.[18] Symbolically, the word reads "weaves" 〰〰〰 "spiritual" 🐦 "knowledge" 🦉 "into time" ⦿, followed by the number 2 ‖ (perhaps a reference to the second house or second stage of matter). The Egyptian concept of knowledge relates to the phoneme *am* or *ama* and so corresponds to the same deity we associate with the second house in the Hindu parable.

We are told that one of the gods "roars with the jaws of a lion." One Egyptian word for "roar" is *nema*.[19] Symbolically, the word reads "weavers of knowledge that is spoken." This phoneme, coupled with the symbolic reference to spoken knowledge, can hardly fail to evoke the concept of the Nummo teachers of the Dogon. An Egyptian word for "the two jaws" is pronounced *skerui*.[20] We have noted that a very similar word, *skheru*, means "chambers." It calls to mind both the eight-chambered stone houses of Skara Brae and the Egyptian word *s-kher*, meaning "to overthrow." The mention of a lion within the tale (defined by an Egyptian word *ru*) seems to assure that we move beyond the simple root phoneme *sker* to the specific word *skeru*, meaning "chambers." Conceptually, we link all of these meanings to the Nem pygmies on Orkney Island, whom we take to be the Nummo teachers of Dogon lore.

The Egyptian tale next conveys an action, telling us that "two figures flash knives." Appropriate to this event, the Egyptian word *neg* can also mean "to cut open, to cut off, or to hew."[21] The root phoneme *neg* means "to lack, to want, to be short of"[22] and so also reflects the underlying theme of successive levels of personal need that we interpreted for the seven Hindu houses.

The spirit next exclaims to the doorkeeper, "You, first being uttered from Temu's teeth!" The applicable Egyptian word for "utterance" is *sma-t*,[23] and it derives from the root *sma*,[24] again meaning "knife" or "sword." The name Temu rests on the cosmological root *tem*, meaning "complete." The image evokes the notion of an original unity, now reconfigured as multiple divisions of matter that will culminate in the formation of a Word.

The spirit calls the watchman a "dog-faced pylon." One Egyptian word for "pylon" or "chamber" is *urit*.[25] Appropriate to that pronunciation, Budge defines the related term *urtt* as "a name for the Other World." In both the Dogon and the Egyptian cosmologies, this Second World, Other World, or Underworld was presided over by a dog-faced jackal, a scavenging animal that was symbolic of the concept of disorder.

Consistent with the symbolic theme of time, the deceased spirit reminisces about how nice it was to be young and talks about eating, sweating, and making love. The notion of eating recalls the act of the second housewife in the Hindu parable, whom Devi finds eating. An Egyptian word meaning "to be young," *uatch*,[26] is a homonym for a word meaning "pillar" or "support."[27] Egyptian words for "sweat" imply the notion of the transmission of water in droplets, comparable to the notion of matter in its wavelike state now dividing into discrete particles. (This image is consonant with another Dogon definition of the word *ie*, given as "to cry with tears.") One Egyptian word for "sweat" is given as *tekheb*.[28] Symbolically, it reads, "reconciliation/union/embrace" ◯ "of the source" ⊜ "in the place of" ⌡ "waves" 〰. The Egyptian word "to make love" is *netchemnetchem*.[29] Symbolically it implies the sexual union between two universes, characterized in the biblical sense as "knowledge": 𓏤 𓅓 𓏤 𓅓 𓂝.

The spirit next observes that "love and anger gave me words of truth." The Egyptian phrase "words of truth" is *metut ent maat*.[30] *Maat*, of course, is the ancient Egyptian term for justice or truth. Symbolically, the phrase reads "perception" ⌡ "gives" ⬭ "mass/matter" ◯ "a voice or a Word" 𓀁. The implied scientific meaning is that an act of perception imparts vibration to mass.

The spirit goes on to say, "But I refined them and I was no less a man of passion for my caution." One Egyptian word for "refined" or "clear" is *stef*.[31] It is a homonym for a word that means "to turn aside" or "to turn away." This is a description of the complex pivoting of matter that, within the context of the cosmology, is understood to occur along with the initial stirrings of matter following an act of perception. (We discussed this aspect of matter and the meanings of related

Egyptian words in chapter 9 of *China's Cosmological Prehistory*.) In keeping with this definition, Dogon cosmological terms that define the stages of matter are referred to as the Clear Word. An alternate Egyptian word for "refined" is *qen*.[32] It is a homonym for a word that means "seat," "throne," and "chair of state" and so, from the matriarchal perspective of the archaic tradition, likely underlies the notion of a queen. The throne is also the icon of goddesses such as Isis in Egypt and Sati in India. The word *qen* is also a homonym for an Egyptian word that refers to a woven mat or carpet, which implies the notion of the weaving of matter.

The Egyptian word for "passion" is *shakaika*.[33] Symbolically, the word characterizes the progressive stages of matter. It reads "reeds" ⦚⦚⦚ "collected" ⌣ "become" 𓅿 "existence" ⦚⦚ "collected" ⌣, "which comes to be" 𓅿 "spoken words" 𓀁⁝. In our view of the Egyptian hieroglyphic language, the word defines the meaning of an unpronounced trailing lotus glyph ⬚.

Next, the traveling spirit states, "The virtues of Thoth made of me more god." One Egyptian word for "virtues" is also the word for "light," *aakhu*.[34] Symbolically, the word reads "that which" 𓏃 "comes" 𓅿 "from the source" ⊜, followed by the light glyph ⦚⦚⦚|. Appropriate to this meaning, our comparative studies have shown that terms for the progressive stages of matter in Dogon cosmology correlate to the names and traditional roles of Egyptian gods. These stages culminate in the formation of a symbolic Word, which is the traditional domain of the Egyptian god Thoth.

The spirit says, "I gave my mind the pleasure of creation." An Egyptian word for "mind" is *ab*,[35] based on a phonetic value that can also mean "heart." One spelling of the word reads "that which is" 𓏃 "the spiritual concept" 𓅜| "of a drop" ⟩. Likewise, an Egyptian word for "pleasure" is *aut ab*,[36] alternately defined as "swelling of the heart." Egyptian concepts of creation rest on the phonetic root *pau*, comparable to the atom-like *po* of the Dogon.

The spirit is quoted as saying, "And the strength of Osiris was the strength of the mind, the strength of the hand, and the strength of will and god." Through our studies in cosmology, we have come to associate the spiral of Barnard's Loop in the macrocosm with Orion/Osiris. That spiral is defined as the counterpart to the spiral of matter, which is the egg of the world. Based on that equivalence and definitions given here, it would be a true symbolic statement to say that the strength of Osiris was the strength of the mind. Egyptian words for "hand" are formed from the same phonetic root *a* that we associate with the Hebrew god Yah. In *Point of Origin,* we correlated the eight incarnations of the elephant god Ganesha to the stages of the egg of the world. An Egyptian word for "will," *ab,*[37] is also found in words that express many of the attributes of Ganesha.

The traveler says, "I am heavy as a stone, not easily blown by the breezes, but I sail when I must and strike a blow to untruth." This statement defines the attributes of mass. The first of these is the notion of weightiness. The next, which defines mass in relation to breezes, uses the cosmological image of wind (vibration) as an opposing attribute to mass. The idea of *striking a blow* exemplifies the notion of a *force,* such as that of gravity, that acts on mass. The Egyptian notion of "untruth," which is *ames,* is given symbolically as "that which interferes with the speaking of the Word." Scientifically speaking, gravity is the force of matter that acts on mass.[38]

The traveler declares himself to be a "priest of light" and a "man of conviction" who has risen up to heaven. In cosmological traditions that closely relate to those of the Dogon, priestly titles such as Hogon (comparable to the Cohane priests of Judaism or the Yoginis in India) traditionally center on phonetic roots that mean "light" and that are often counterparts to the Dogon word *ogo* and the Egyptian word *aakhu.* Ogo is also the name of a character in Dogon myth whose conviction to create a universe as perfect as the creator god Amma's causes him to rise up and results in the formation of space.

THE THIRD HOUSE

When the spirit traveler reaches the third house, he finds three gods dancing in the doorway. An Egyptian word for "dance" is *abu*,[39] and it is a word that we associate with attributes of the elephant god Ganesha. Homonyms for the word carry meanings that encompass a number of icons or attributes of Ganesha. These include the meanings of "elephant," "tusk," and "scepter," as well as the notion of dancing itself.

We are told that two of the gods of the third house are wearing the snouts of a jackal. The Egyptian word for "snout" is *khenti*,[40] and the same word means "the first," "chief," and "he who is at the head." Ganesha, whose mythical role was as a doorkeeper for his mother Sati, is traditionally viewed as the god of beginnings and the lord of the *ganas*—the multitudes who served as the retinue of the god Siva/Shiva. In *Point of Origin*, we discussed the symbolic relationship between the Dogon egg of the world and the action of a sieve, which is the cosmological concept we interpret the god Siva to represent. The third god of the house was said to spin "round and round about a stalk of corn." Spinning is again a signature attribute of Ganesha, who is said to dance and spin on one leg. The Egyptian word for "stalk" is *ar-t*,[41] a phonetic equivalent for the term *arit*, which defines the seven dimensions symbolized by the houses of the tale—the same dimensions for which Ganesha acts as gatekeeper.

The spirit hurls insults and declarations at the three gods. He refers to the watchman as "uplifting his face" and to the herald's "voice of thunder." An Egyptian word for "voice" is *kheru*, and a term meaning "the sound of thunder" is given as *kheru em pet*.[42] Within our system of cosmology, the term *pet* refers to the notion of space. The spirit demands that the three gods "let the shadow of an old man pass!" An Egyptian word for "shadow" is *khaib-t*, based on a phonetic root *khai*, which means "to lift up."[43] The cosmological implication of these combined references is that vibrations of matter lift mass upward to create the concept of space.

The spirit makes a series of characterizations of his own state of being, describing himself as "hidden in the deep" and as "a form in the green ocean of being." He states that "light leaps up like the two white horns of a bull." One common thread to his statements is that they all relate to the notion of the existence of differentiated forms in the unseen microcosm of matter. The Egyptian words evoked by this series of statements center on the term *meskh-t*.[44] According to Budge, the similar term *Meskh-ti* is the name of a bull-headed constellation with seven stars and so conjures images of the Dogon egg of the world, conceptualized as seven rays of a star.

THE FOURTH HOUSE

When the traveling spirit arrives at the fourth house, he finds three gods shimmering in the doorway. The Egyptian word for "shimmer" is *beqa,* and according to Budge, the same word also means "light."[45] One of the gods is a "golden hawk soaring." Budge lists a term for "hawk of gold" that is pronounced *bak*[46]—a rough phonetic equivalent to the term *beqa.* The word for "soar" is *akh,*[47] a phonetic root that means "light." We are told that one beast "wears the face of a man, one the face of a lion." Terms for both "man" and "lion" are formed on the phonetic root *rem*.[48] The term *remen* refers to the cubit as a unit of measure.[49] Another term for "cubit" is *aakhu meh,* a designation that is founded on a phonetic root that also means "light."

The spirit cries out, "You, doorkeeper, great of speech but repulsive of face!" Egyptian terms for "speech" and the notion of repulsing an enemy in the context of a rebellion rest on a phonetic root *sheb*.[50] Words founded on the same phonetic value also imply fighting, the act that the goddess Devi finds in the fourth house of the Hindu parable.

The traveler exclaims, "I am a spirit." An Egyptian word for "spirit" is *aakhu,*[51] a word that also means "light." The spirit declares himself to be an ox. An Egyptian word for ox is *aa,*[52] the same phonetic value we associate with the Hebrew god of light, Yah. The spirit defines himself as "the son of limitless earth and sky." The Egyptian term for "limitless" is *tcher* or *tcheru*.[53] From the perspective of our cosmology, limitlessness is a concept that pertains to the nonmaterial universe, which is of the nature of light.

He states, "I am the heart of Osiris, pillar of my mother's house, light of my father." Egyptian words for "heart"[54] and "father"[55] are founded on the phonetic root *ab* and so again imply a relationship to the elephant god Ganesha. The traveler calls himself "a scribe faithful to the language of the heart." Many of the titles applied to scribes begin with the phonetic value *sesh*[56] and so are reflective of the goddess Seshat's authority (centered at Abydos during dynastic times) over scribes and inscriptions.

The spirit is quoted as saying, "I am a man born under fortunate stars into the hands of gods and goddesses. I have cut loose my body. I have risen up and walked about heaven." These references repeat episodes from the myth of the elephant god Ganesha, who was fashioned from clay by his goddess mother, Sati, who then breathed life into him (thus he was born into her hands). His original head was said to have been mistakenly cut off by the god Siva (thus cutting loose his body). Siva replaced his head with the head of a white elephant (thus he "rose up" or was reanimated). The Egyptian term "walk about" is expressed by the word *reh*,[57] which can also mean "care" or "anxiety," which are among the kinds of obstacles that Ganesha is often entreated to relieve by his parishioners. The spirit also specifically asserts, "I rise from the egg of the world," a statement that places the symbolism of the spirit's travels squarely in the symbolic arena that we have proposed and also squarely in the domain of Ganesha as we understand his symbolism. In *Point of Origin*, we devoted a chapter to discussing the eight incarnations of Ganesha, which, in our view, correlate to progressive stages of the creation of matter that define the egg of the world. Last, the spirit describes himself as "light sailing on air." From a cosmological perspective, the egg of the world constitutes a spiral that entwines light from the nonmaterial universe with vibrations of mass from the material universe, which are characterized as wind and air.

THE FIFTH HOUSE

At the fifth house, three gods guard the doorway. The likely related Egyptian word for "guard" is *asa*,[58] which is the phonetic root of the name of the god Asar/Osiris. Symbolically, the word reads "binding" ⎯∞⎯ "comes to be" 𓅃 .

One of the three gods "sprouts the wings and beak of a hawk." These are likely references to the Egyptian god Horus, who was the mythical son of Osiris and Isis, much the same as Ganesha was the son of Siva and Sati in India.

One of the gods has "the head of seven writhing snakes." An Egyptian word for "snake" is *aar-t*,[59] a phonetic equivalent to the term *arit*, which we associate with the seven spiraling divisions of the egg of the world. Each god holds a knife. An alternate Egyptian word for "knife" is *ari*.[60]

The spirit cries out, "You doorkeeper! Groveling in the dirt, living on worms!" Egyptian words for "grovel" and "dirt" are formed from the phonetic root Heb,[61] which Budge defines as the name of a now little-known god who, like Ganesha and Horus, was the son of a creator god.

The deceased spirit cries, "You, watchman, you pool of fire!" An Egyptian term for "liquid fire in the Tuat" is *netu*,[62] which calls to mind the Egyptian goddess Net/Neith—the same deity we associate with symbolic levels of need and the seven Hindu houses. The spirit cries, "You, herald, with the hippo face, falling down before god!" An Egyptian word for "hippopotamus" is *nehes*,[63] comparable to the Egyptian word *nehet*, meaning "need."

THE SIXTH HOUSE

Arriving at the sixth house, the spirit finds three gods sleeping. A likely Egyptian correlate is to the word *aun*, which means "to sleep."[64] The word is also given unspecifically by Budge as the name of "an Egyptian god." Symbolically, the name reads "the force of" ⎯⎯ "vibrations" 𓂓 𓈖.

The text enigmatically states, "Three dogs, three tongues lolling, three bellies drunk with meat." An Egyptian word for "dog" is *auau*,[65] a word that may reflect the sound a dog makes. The cosmological reference is to the opening of a dog's mouth in the shape of "<", and the implication is one of vibration growing and mass rising up. Budge includes a dictionary entry for the related phonetic root *au*,[66] which means "to be spacious" and refers to "the height of a spirit." The word *lolling* implies the notion of stretching out in a relaxed and lazy manner. A comparable Egyptian term is *aui*,[67] which means "to stretch out" or "extend." The Egyptian word for "drunk" is *nuh*,[68] a homonym for another word *nuh*,[69] which means "string." From a cosmological perspective, matter is the product of the vibration of primordial strings.

The spirit says, "I have come like the sun bursting forth on the first day." In both a cosmological and scientific view, the Egyptian sun glyph ⊙ represents the first discrete shape that appears during the processes of creation. He says, "I have kept my eye on the path, the winding secret ways through the mountain." Again cosmologically, the stages of formation of matter are conceptualized as a winding spiral, and the raising up of matter is compared metaphorically to a mountain.

The spirit says, "I have left behind what was made of nature, the body of earth, the clay, the water." An Egyptian word for "nature" is *ami-t*,[70] and it refers symbolically to the previously cited notion of drops of water that, conceptually, would be intermediate between matter in its wavelike state and matter in a solid state. We understand the phrase "body of earth" to refer symbolically to the concept of mass. Likewise, clay is a substance that falls conceptually between water and solid earth.

The spirit says, "I carry the crown of existence." The concept of existence is conveyed by the Egyptian word *skher*,[71] which is a cosmological reference to the egg of the world and in our view is symbolized by Skara Brae. Similarly, an Egyptian word for "crown" is *skhen-t*.[72]

The spirit claims to have become the man he was "through determination to walk in truth and light." An Egyptian term for "truth" is *bu maa*,[73] a counterpart to the Dogon concept of bummo. This implies the notion of an act of perception that catalyzes the formation of matter through an embrace with light. He says, "I have seen the great world and the small world." These are references to the concepts of the macrocosm and the microcosm, and so exemplify the principal theme of the cosmology: as above, so below.

THE SEVENTH HOUSE

From the cosmological perspective of the Dogon, the seventh chamber of the egg of the world completes the egg. In this Egyptian tale of the "Seven Houses in the Other World," we are told, "The road twists and curls and twines." These are defined attributes of the egg of the world, the spiral of matter that conceptually intertwines the feminine energy of the nonmaterial universe (light) with the masculine energy of the material universe (mass) to create the reality we perceive. We are told, "The road rears up. It is the head of a snake." The cosmological concept that is conveyed here is that of the ascension of matter. An Egyptian word for "to rise up, to ascend, to rear" is *hi*.[74] Symbolically, the word reads "the entwined dimensions" ⚇ "exist" ⊓⊓, followed by the walking feet glyph ⩕. In our view of the Egyptian hieroglyphic language, the image of the rearing serpent ⌇ represents the concept of the Word, a term the Dogon apply to their completed egg as the first discrete unit of matter.

The spirit says, "I walk past the two obelisks of its teeth." For us, the two obelisks, reminiscent of the two standing stones that frame the image of Maes Howe from Stenness, are counterparts to two written reedleaf glyphs ⊓⊓ and so represent the concept of existence. An Egyptian word for "teeth," *behu*,[75] is formed from a phonetic root *beh* that also means "to cut or hew stone."

As the spirit arrives at the seventh house, we are told, "Three gods lock hands inside the doorway." The image of locked hands recalls the concept of the embrace between the nonmaterial and material universes that characterizes the egg of the world in the ancient cosmology. It also evokes the notion of "grasping and holding firm" that alternately defines the "hidden gods" of our tradition, such as Amma and Amen.

We are told, "The lion and the hare cross lances against me." An Egyptian word for "lance" is *ua*,[76] a word for "lion" is *ua-ti*,[77] and a word for "hare" is *un* or *un-t*.[78] Budge defines the word Ua,[79] meaning "the One," as a title both for Amen and for "the deceased as a divine being." He cites Pepi II, the pharaoh who was said to have worked in the Field of Reeds in a passage from *The Egyptian Book of the Dead*, as an example. Clearly the term "the One" also pertains sensibly to the egg of the world itself, as the first finished structure of matter.

We are told, "The old man between the guardians smiles. He resembles me." An Egyptian word for "resemble" is *neher*,[80] and the word *neherneher* means "rejoice." Both words call to mind the Egyptian word for "need," *nehet*, and the name of the mother goddess Net/Neith, who weaves matter. However, an Egyptian word for "smile," *sebt*,[81] conjures the number seven—the number of stages of the egg of the world and the number of the house in which its symbolism is given. It is interesting that another Egyptian word for "smile," *sabi*,[82] is formed from the root *sab*, which means "jackal." The suggestion is that the jackal becomes the symbolic guardian of the Egyptian Underworld and Dogon Second World of matter partly because the word for "jackal" implies the number seven.

We are told of the old man that "his two hands hold ears of corn." An Egyptian word for "ear of corn" is *khemes*,[83] which is phonetically similar to the word *khemen-t*, meaning "shrine." From a cosmological perspective, the stupa shrine represents the grand symbol of the egg of the world. Likewise, the symbolism of the base plan of the stupa (the egg in a ball) evokes a series of symbolic pairs of opposing elements that we associate with the eight paired deities who emerge in two cosmological constructs of ancient Egypt, known as the Ogdoad and Ennead, discussed in previous volumes of this series. So it seems significant that Khemenu is a name for a group of eight Egyptian elemental deities,[84] just as Khemet was an ancient name for Egypt itself.

The spirit cries, "You, doorkeeper, with the sharp, slashing knife! You, watchman, carrying my own face! You, herald, with words sharp as a knife!" An Egyptian word that means "sharp like a knife" is *m'tes*.[85] Words from the same phonetic root imply the notion of a road, way, or path (symbolically, we infer an intended meaning of "end of a road, way, or path"), along with the idea of an inscription that has now been written.

At this point, the spirit claims to be "Osiris, pure in emanation. . . . I have cut loose my body. I walk about stars. I sail the heavens with gods. I hold long conversations with beings of light." These statements suggest that notions of the ascension of a deceased pharaoh who becomes a star should be understood in relation to cosmological processes of the ascension or emanation of matter. They also reaffirm the idea that these processes represent an interface between a nonmaterial realm characterized as light and our material realm.

Appropriate to this outlook, the Egyptian name for Osiris, Asar,[86] is written symbolically as "throne" ⌐ "of perception" ◁◇. Much as the ancient cosmology asserts that a perfect reality in its wavelike state is disrupted by an act of perception and then reorganized into the matter as we know it, so Osiris was said to have been dismembered and then ultimately reconstituted to become, as Budge notes, the king of the dead.

Our outlook on the Skara Brae site is that it links symbolically to the Dogon and Egyptian cosmologies first through the architecture of the stone houses, which, according to Dogon sources, is meant to represent a sleeping woman. We infer this to be the same sleeping goddess who is more overtly referred to in the traditions of various cultures as foundational to the processes of material creation. In our view, the series of megalithic sites on Orkney Island that lead us to Skara Brae constitute a life-size representation of the stages of creation in the Dogon Second World of matter, a cosmological realm that we associate with the Egyptian Underworld. Moreover, a variety of Dogon, Egyptian, and ancient Greek references serve to specifically associate Orkney Island with ancient concepts of the Underworld, which we relate to seven progressive stages of matter that are characterized by the Dogon as chambers. So it seems significant that the language of two ancient myths, framed in relation to seven houses, deities, a deceased spirit, and a journey through the Underworld, plays out in consistent relation to key words and themes of this same cosmological tradition.

23
CONCLUSIONS
AND OBSERVATIONS

When I was new to the study of Egyptian culture, religion, and language, the sources I worked with presented me with a somewhat bewildering array of symbolic images, deities, architectural forms, societal practices, and word forms. (One comedian jokes, "It's like they had a different word for *everything!*") But in truth, the situation was more complicated than that. There appeared to be multiple, seemingly unrelated words to express any given concept, written with glyphs whose images seemed, at best, enigmatic. Furthermore, each word had multiple homonyms that seemed to express widely differing meanings. Nor often was there simply one glyph to express a given concept. It was as if someone had intermingled references from two or more conceptually compatible but outwardly dissimilar traditions.

Over the course of our studies, it has become clear that, between the archaic period and historical times, certain widespread reversals in symbolism occurred in the cosmologies of various ancient cultures. Perhaps the clearest example of this kind of reversal is the apparent sublimation of what in archaic time was a matriarchal tradition by a later tradition in which creator gods largely predominated. At the same time, a system of cosmology that had been successfully passed down mnemonically through the generations as an oral tradition now began to be set down in written symbols.

However, there were also many other overt changes in symbolism that seemingly took place, on which we have commented over the course of this series, sometimes with a hint of tentative confusion. The fact that these changes seem to have taken effect not for just one single culture but in a synchronous way for sometimes widely distant cultures during the same era suggests behind-the-scenes action of some globally capable influence. Based on our studies, we now understand this to reflect what we interpret as the occasionally revealed hand of a group of ancestor-teachers.

Because these reversals appeared hand in hand with the introduction of written language, we have few surviving texts by which to anchor them. However, certain attributes of Abydos, given in relation to its establishment as the original seat of pharaonic rule in Egypt, provide us with clear evidence of this transition and for perhaps the first time point to a specific era in which many of these changes may have transpired. At Abydos we see the establishment of an ordered civilization in ancient Egypt, but one that was apparently overlaid on preexisting elements of an archaic tradition.

Some researchers, including my good friend John Anthony West, argue that ancient Egyptian culture was a legacy—a remnant of a higher civilization that existed and was ultimately destroyed sometime prior to the last ice age. If we allow for that possibility, then aspects of what we see in ancient Egyptian culture may reflect influences that are tens of thousands of years old.

If we entertain the idea that the Sphinx and the three largest pyramids at Giza exhibit alignments to astronomical bodies as they were positioned in the era of 10,000 BCE, as my friend Robert Bauval proposes, then as researchers we are left with only two possibilities: Either the alignments were set down in the era of 10,000 BCE, or some later culture must have been capable of calculating the proper alignments retrospectively. The suggestion, based on this and other evidence such as the Egyptian king lists, is that these monuments might reflect influences on Egypt at around 10,000 BCE.

We additionally see that a Sakti-like tradition took hold in Egypt during predynastic times (at or before 4000 BCE—some think *long* before), and we can point to evidence of it in at least two distinct locales, both of which have legitimate claim to archaic roots. These are the island of Elephantine and the ancient stone quarries of Gebel el Silsila. It seems likely that this same matriarchal tradition also took root in Nubia to the south. (In accordance with an ancient naming convention for tribes of our tradition, the Egyptian name Nubia can be interpreted to combine the words *Nu* and *bia,* meaning "Nu is wonderful.") We also know based on the Two Ladies endorsement of Menes during the era of the First Dynasty that both Upper and Lower Egypt had celebrated mother goddesses in the period immediately preceding predynastic times, so any newly established king may have required their endorsement to affirm his own legitimacy.

The archaic tradition we place at Elephantine expressed itself in relation to two archaic Egyptian mother goddesses, Satet and Anuket, and a popular Ganesha-like deity of the Nile inundation and of agricultural abundance named Hapy. The two goddesses were likely counterparts to Tana Penu and Dharni Penu in India and to Isis and Nephthys in dynastic Egypt. We also know that Egyptian references to an archaic First Time are sometimes given in relation to an earth god called Tanen, whose name shares a phonetic root with the Sakti earth goddess Tana Penu. Many of the iconic elements of the Sakti tradition were overtly evident in archaic times at Elephantine, most notably in the form of the elephant and single-tusk symbolism that originally defined the locale, but also in relation to traditional icons of the two sister goddesses, such as clay pots known as potbellies. The significance of these elements of the matriarchal tradition seems to have largely faded from prominence after the transition to a patriarchal tradition sometime later during dynastic times.

A thousand or more years later, rule was established at Abydos, a city (and region) whose name, *abu,* was based on a phonetic root *aab,* which means "scepter." The scepter, we know, was an icon of Ganesha in India. The same phoneme also forms the root of a name of Elephantine and of Egyptian words for "elephant" and "tusk," which Budge also gives as *abu*. Indications are that the goddess Seshat was celebrated at Abydos since at least the beginning of dynastic times, but that centuries may have transpired before male deities of the patriarchal tradition, such as Osiris and Horus, ultimately rose to ascendance there.

Barry J. Kemp cites "an elusive geographical background to the cult of Horus,"[1] suggesting that traditional Egyptologists are not entirely certain how or where the tradition evolved. He writes, "We are not justified in drawing the conclusion that there had been in very early times an important centre for Horus in the North. All the unambiguous textual references are no earlier than the late Old Kingdom. Some 500 years separate this time from the period of state formation in Egypt, and it was during this interval that the basic shape of Pharaonic court culture was formalized. The process was a dynamic one, involving a systematizing of myth, which surfaces eventually in the Pyramid Texts . . . [at] the end of the 5th Dynasty onwards."[2]

The Egyptian symbol for Horus was a falcon, which is traditionally deemed to have represented the lanner or peregrine falcon species. The peregrine is found in many widespread regions of the world, including the Faroe and Orkney Islands. The Egyptian term is often reconstructed phonetically as *hāru* and so reflects the same *arou* or *aaru* root that we associate with Orkney Island and the Field of Reeds. At the earliest, worship of Horus in Egypt dates from the same predynastic era as Skara Brae, around 3200 BCE. The suggestion is that the cult of Horus arose in Egypt as an aspect of dynastic kingship and of our postulated reformulation of the ancient cosmology.

At Abydos, in conjunction with the establishment of dynastic kingship, emphasis was placed on a goddess named Seshat. Her name was based on the phonetic root *seh*, which refers to a portable ritual shrine that Kemp says represented a kind of prototype for ancient Egyptian architectural forms. Based on her icons, known symbolism, and surviving references in Egyptian language, texts, and art, Seshat effectively combined many of the key symbolic elements of the cosmology and civilizing plan. She had authority over the alignment of shrines, which represents the conceptual starting point of our cosmology. Her signature glyph combines cosmological elements of the Dogon egg of the world with biological elements and so unites at least two creational themes of the cosmology. Seshat's domain was the written word, inscriptions, and instructed knowledge, which linked her conceptually to the ancestor-teachers and to the mythical givers of written language in Egypt. Traditional researchers assign her a pivotal role in funerary rituals that link her to the concept of the Egyptian Underworld and by extension to the Dogon Second World of matter. She played a critical role in the recertification of Egyptian pharaohs and so was intimately linked with the establishment of kingship in Egypt and with the place of its establishment, Abydos. Looked at in this way, Seshat effectively consolidated many of the diverse cosmological roles of ancient mother goddesses into a single Egyptian goddess, and did so explicitly in relation to the establishment of dynastic kingship.

Also evident in this later tradition of dynastic Egypt were mythical themes that carried forward from the archaic tradition, most notably the story of a deity who was dismembered, whose body parts were scattered to all parts of the region, and who was ultimately reconstituted. However, from dynastic times forward in Egypt these themes were associated with a creator god, Osiris, not a mother goddess. From the standpoint of dynastic Egypt, Osiris stood in the place of the Indian goddess Sati in the rendition of the dismemberment myth. Similarly, in the earliest traditions in China, it is the goddess Nu-Wa who creates mankind from clay, much as Sati was said to fashion an initially human son, Ganesha, from clay in India. But by the era of the predynastic/dynastic boundary, this act of biological creation begins to fall to male gods comparable to the Dogon god Amma, who are credited with having created humanity from clay.

All of these elements seem to reflect major revisions in how the system of cosmology was framed in relation to humanity. Dogon culture as we understand it appears to have separated from Egypt at around this same point of transition, just before the introduction of written language and just before many of the reversals in symbolism were fully implemented. It is during this era that we would expect to find the transition from three-stone cairns (like the one originally found at the center of the Stenness stone circle) to Dogon granary-like stupas. In support of this view, the Dogon retain both forms. Much like the concept of the composite mother goddess Seshat, we interpret the Dogon granary as a carefully conceived symbol of a reconstituted cosmology, one that reflects certain transitional differences when compared to a Buddhist stupa. Linguistically, it is clear that Dogon society descended from an archaic tradition associated with the Dravidians and the Sakti cult, since we find Dravidian word forms in the Dogon language. We see this same line of descent as one of the likely sources of predynastic culture in ancient Egypt.

The Sphinx, which is understood to have been carved from a natural stone outcropping, exemplifies one signature practice of the archaic tradition and signals, with its leonid form and its apparent astronomic relationship to the period of 10,000 BCE, an intention (if not more likely an actual attempt) on the part of the archaic ancestor-teachers to establish an agriculturally based civilization in Egypt. The suggestion is that this culture, which seems to have also produced predynastic kingships, somehow failed to cohere in the ways originally intended by those teachers.

In that light, Orkney Island would seem to reflect a secondary attempt to impart knowledge to humanity, with the specific goal of establishing regional kingships, all founded on a self-sustaining system of agriculture, at the four cardinal points of the compass. These would have been Egypt (Taru), Ireland (Aaru), China (Iru), and Peru (Peru). Timing of the construction of the passage tomb at Newgrange, which is dated to around 3200 BCE—the same era as the Orkney Island structures—suggests that Ireland, which was geographically nearest to the Orkney and Faroe Islands, came first in this secondary effort.

The few details we have relating to inhabitants found on Orkney

Island in ancient times suggest that they consisted of a group of dark-complexioned or otherwise racially distinct priestly clerics who dressed in white, comparable to the Dogon priests, and these clerics interacted with a group of pygmies who displayed odd habits and were capable of overcoming, capturing, and transporting a troop of hardy Mediterranean explorers twice their size; in fact, the explorers specifically described their smaller captors as sorcerers. These descriptions, along with the Egyptian *nem* and *nemma* words for "pygmy," suggest that these small people may have been the mythical Nummo teachers of Dogon agriculture and cosmology.

To secure their own safe haven during these times of secondary instruction, it makes sense that these ancestor-teachers would have established themselves in the Faroe Islands. Unexcavated structures exist in the Faroe Islands that look outwardly pyramidal in shape and could reflect the hand of the teachers in many of the same ways as the Great Pyramid of Egypt. The term *faro,* which designated the home of these ancestor-teachers, was adopted by the first kings of Egypt as a term for their palaces, which Budge gives as *per-aa.* The word is interpreted to mean "great house" but was written symbolically as "structure" $\boxed{}$ "of authority" ⟨⟩.[3] Later, the term was applied by association to the Egyptian pharaohs themselves and (according to Budge) was sometimes adopted even by mere officers of the king.

We interpret the megalithic structures on Orkney Island both as composing an instructional sanctuary that enshrined the stages of creation and as part of ongoing, hands-on projects for a series of groups of initiates. The suggestion is that each group of initiates may have been assigned to complete the next successive phase of long-term projects that were deliberately extended over time. In this view, the final graduating class that should have completed the mysteriously unfinished stone circle at Stenness was somehow never able to do so. Perhaps the last planned training session was canceled, or it may have been unexpectedly abrupted in its process. In dynastic Egypt, we see this same tradition of megalithic construction based on what appears to have been a specific, well-conceived, preexisting plan, carried out over an extended period of time by a succession of pharaonic rulers.

From this perspective, the village of Skara Brae would have essentially constituted dorm housing for instructed groups of eight initiates and perhaps their families, the same number per group of initiates as is claimed by the Dogon priests and the same number of ancestral families that the Dogon traditionally honor. The evidence, based on the phonetic commonality of names like Lebe and Levi, assigned to honored ancestral families by the Dogon and in Judaism, is that a similar set of ancestral families were honored in those traditions.

The cosmology associated with a Dogon house is overtly apparent at Skara Brae and seems to be reflected linguistically in the Faroese language. The symbolism of the structure of the Skara Brae house, which the Dogon assert is based on the major structures of the human body, is consistent with what R. A. Schwaller de Lubicz interprets for the Egyptian Temple of Man at Luxor. From this perspective, the central hearth that is found in homes at Skara Brae would have constituted an original feature of the plan but was later omitted by the Dogon because of the relatively hot climate of their desert locale, rather than (as we initially surmised) being a feature added after the fact, curiously in symbolic harmony with the Dogon plan, by the inhabitants of Skara Brae.

Like the Skara Brae house plan, the plan of the village set a working pattern that has largely survived down through the centuries as the Dogon village. The village also gave the initiates immediate access to a functioning model farm, which the Dogon call the Field of Arou, where they practiced and mastered skills of farming. Evidence of domesticated animals near Skara Brae suggests instruction in animal husbandry also occurred there. From this perspective, life on Orkney Island would have constituted something like the college experience that modern students enjoy and would have set the pattern for the kind of idealized lifestyle that modern students are often reluctant to move on from after graduation. As such, it seems understandable that Orkney Island might have been adopted by the Egyptians as the pattern for an afterlife.

Associations between the concept of the Elysian Fields (the Egyptian Field of Reeds) and Abydos provide another suggestive link between the dynastic kingship in Egypt and Orkney Island. By the time of the ancient Greeks, the Elysian Fields were understood as a place where honored heroes were buried so that they could be close to the gods. Abydos was seen by the Egyptian elite to have similar afterlife associations. From the time of the early dynasties in Egypt, actual or symbolic burial at Abydos was looked on as a guarantee of close association with the gods.

Passages from *The Egyptian Book of the Dead,* which indicate that after death Pepi would be required to do work in a field, show that the Egyptian concept of the Field of Reeds specifically identified the mythical locale with an agricultural field. This is consonant with the Dogon usage, where the Field of Arou represented both a cosmological background field for fundamental particles of matter and an actual, physically cultivated agricultural field. Likewise, we have argued in previous volumes that the Dogon Second World of matter, where these fundamental particles form, is a conceptual counterpart to the Egyptian Underworld, or Tuat. If we can interpret descriptions of Pepi and the Field of Reeds as geographically correct references to Orkney Island, then the suggestion is that we may need to reconsider both *The Egyptian Book of the Dead* and the very similar *Tibetan Book of the Dead* in an entirely new light, since these new associations imply that what has long been taken to be mythical may in actuality have important historical aspects.

One important detail to be drawn from the comparisons of this study is to note that, as with tales of the city of Troy and the Trojan War that were later demonstrated by Heinrich Schliemann to be historical and factual, it seems once again that we can trust the claims of the ancient Greek writers, who consistently relayed factual details in their descriptions of the Elysian Fields. This suggests that they may have also been factually correct in their view that dignitaries of ancient Egypt were actually sent to be buried at Maes Howe, so as to be in the proximity of the ancestor-teachers. It also supports the notion that the ancestor-teachers had permanently located themselves near Orkney Island. Moreover, based on the apparent truthfulness of these reports, it might behoove us to reenergize our efforts to interpret the seemingly mythical Greek tales of Atlantis, a land that was said to have been located in the middle of the True Ocean, across from the Pillars of Hercules, a reference that we take to mean Gibraltar.

As a final observation, a historical derivation for the name of Scotland remains uncertain. We know that it did not come out of Latin, and it also does not relate to any known term used by the Gaelic tribes to describe themselves. Several speculative suggestions have been put forth regarding an origin for the word, but to date none of these has gained general acceptance. However, we understand based on our discussion here that Northern Scotland was known to the ancient Egyptians and Greeks as the mythical home of a life-size model of the egg of the world. Take it from a Laird, it seems more than coincidental that a proper cosmological term for that structure was *s-khet*. Given that, does it not seem reasonable that they would have conceived of the Orkney region as S-khet-land?

NOTES

CHAPTER 1.
A BRIEF HISTORY
OF SKARA BRAE

1. Childe and Clarke, *Skara Brae,* 5–6.
2. Arnold, *Stone Age Farmers,* 11.
3. Childe and Clarke, *Skara Brae,* 6.
4. BBC, "Scotland's History."
5. Ibid.
6. National Library of Scotland, *Blaeu Atlas of Scotland,* 1654.
7. Barnes, *Norn Language,* 4.
8. Parker, *Webster's Faroese-English Thesaurus Dictionary,* 229.

CHAPTER 3.
REEXAMINING SKARA BRAE
IN OVERVIEW

1. Calame-Griaule, *Dictionnaire Dogon,* 215.
2. Budge, *Egyptian Hieroglyphic Dictionary,* 233b.
3. BBC, "Scotland's History."
4. "Study Reveals 'Extraordinary' DNA of People in Scotland," BBC News, www.bbc.com/news/uk-scotland-17740638 (accessed August 16, 2016).
5. Higgins, "Scottish People's DNA Study."
6. Mann, "Vikings, Merchants and Pirates."

CHAPTER 4.
COMPARING SKARA BRAE AND DOGON STRUCTURES

1. Dunrea, *Skara Brae,* illustration approximately 11 pages in.
2. Budge, *Egyptian Hieroglyphic Dictionary,* 521b–522a.
3. Parker, *Webster's Faroese-English Thesaurus Dictionary,* 93b.
4. Calame-Griaule, *Dictionnaire Dogon,* 95.
5. Parker, *Webster's Faroese-English Thesaurus Dictionary,* 385a.
6. Ibid., 382b.
7. Budge, *Egyptian Hieroglyphic Dictionary,* 516b.
8. Ibid., 517a.
9. Calame-Griaule, *Dictionnaire Dogon,* 320a, 319a.
10. Parker, *Webster's Faroese-English Thesaurus Dictionary,* 333b.

CHAPTER 5.
DOGON, EGYPTIAN, AND
FAROESE WORDS OF COSMOLOGY

1. Parker, *Webster's Faroese-English Thesaurus Dictionary,* 214b.
2. Ibid., 203a.
3. Ibid., 69a.
4. Ibid., 230b.
5. Ibid., 36a.
6. Budge, *Egyptian Hieroglyphic Dictionary,* 694–95.
7. Parker, *Webster's Faroese-English Thesaurus Dictionary,* 390a.
8. Ibid., 269b.
9. Ibid., 257b.

CHAPTER 6.
COSMOLOGICAL SITES OF THE ORKNEY REGION

1. *Merriam-Webster Dictionary,* s.v. "Ness," www.merriam-webster.com/dictionary /ness (accessed May 2, 2016).
2. Budge, *Egyptian Hieroglyphic Dictionary,* 389b–390a.
3. Ibid., 351b.
4. Parker, *Webster's Faroese-English Thesaurus Dictionary,* 214a.
5. Budge, *Egyptian Hieroglyphic Dictionary,* 442a.

6. Parker, *Webster's Faroese-English Thesaurus Dictionary*, 269–70.

7. Ibid., 432b.

8. Barry, *History of the Orkney Islands*, 30.

9. Richards, *Building the Great Stone Circles*, 70.

10. Ibid., 74.

11. Budge, *Egyptian Hieroglyphic Dictionary*, 711a.

12. Ibid., 321ab.

13. Calame-Griaule, *Dictionnaire Dogon*, 185.

14. *Merriam-Webster Dictionary*, s.v. "Howe," www.merriam-webster.com/dictionary /howe (accessed May 2, 2016).

15. Budge, *Egyptian Hieroglyphic Dictionary*, 440a.

16. Ibid., 617b.

17. Thornhill, "'Discovery of a Lifetime.'"

CHAPTER 7. THE DOGON FIELD OF AROU

1. Parker, *Webster's Faroese-English Thesaurus Dictionary*, 126b.

2. Griaule and Dieterlen, *Pale Fox*, 106–9.

3. Calame-Griaule, *Dictionnaire Dogon*, 14.

4. Parker, *Webster's Faroese-English Thesaurus Dictionary*, 14b.

5. Budge, *Egyptian Hieroglyphic Dictionary*, 65a.

6. Ibid., 130b.

7. Ibid., 21a.

8. Ibid., 21b.

CHAPTER 8.
THE FIELD OF AROU AND THE ELYSIAN FIELDS

1. Budge, *Egyptian Hieroglyphic Dictionary*, 686a.

2. Ibid., 1035b.

3. Ibid., 21b.

4. *Encyclopædia Britannica*, s.v. "Elysium," www.britannica.com/EBchecked /topic/185418/Elysium (accessed May 2, 2016).

5. Budge, *Egyptian Hieroglyphic Dictionary*, 273ab.

6. Parker, *Webster's Faroese-English Thesaurus Dictionary*, 257b.

7. Ibid., 123a.

8. Redford, *Ancient Gods Speak*, 310–11.

9. Ibid., 4.

10. Frankfort, *Ancient Egyptian Religion*, 112.

11. Ibid., 110.

12. Cenival and Pierrat-Bonnefois, "Fragment of the *Book of the Dead*."

13. Orkneyjar, "Climate of Orkney."

14. Parker, *Webster's Faroese-English Thesaurus Dictionary*, 13a.

15. Ibid., 221a.

CHAPTER 9.
FURTHER CORRELATIONS TO FAROESE WORDS

1. Parker, *Webster's Faroese-English Thesaurus Dictionary*, 62a.

2. Ibid., 149b.

3. Ibid., 67b.

4. Ibid., 67a.

5. Ibid., 292.

6. Budge, *Egyptian Hieroglyphic Dictionary*, 671a.

7. Parker, *Webster's Faroese-English Thesaurus Dictionary*, 346a.

8. Ibid., 347a.

9. Ibid., 227a.

10. Ibid., 214b.

11. Ibid., 428b.

12. Ibid., 322b.

CHAPTER 10. ARGAT:
AN ANCIENT NAME FOR ORKNEY ISLAND

1. Budge, *Egyptian Hieroglyphic Dictionary*, 129a.

2. Ibid., 130a.

3. Woodlief, "Story of Orpheus and Eurydice."

4. Theoi Greek Mythology, "Realm of Elysion."

5. Parker, *Webster's Faroese-English Thesaurus Dictionary*, 109a.

6. Theoi Greek Mythology, "Realm of Elysion."

7. Homer, *Odyssey*, www.theoi.com/Kosmos/Elysion.html (accessed June 15, 2016).

8. Parker, *Webster's Faroese-English Thesaurus Dictionary*, 258b.

9. Budge, *Egyptian Hieroglyphic Dictionary*, 652a.

10. Ibid., 131b.

11. Pritchard, *Ancient Near-Eastern Texts*, 33.

12. Budge, *Egyptian Hieroglyphic Dictionary*, 1013b.

13. Parker, *Webster's Faroese-English Thesaurus Dictionary*, 148b.

CHAPTER 11.
ORKNEY ISLAND AS AN ARCHAIC SANCTUARY

1. Ritchie, *Scotland BC*, 11.

2. Budge, *Egyptian Hieroglyphic Dictionary*, 131.

3. Ibid., 462b.

4. Ibid., 651b.

CHAPTER 12.
THE OVERTHROWN BOAT

1. Calame-Griaule, *Dictionnaire Dogon*, 89.

2. Budge, *Egyptian Hieroglyphic Dictionary*, 800b.

3. Ibid., 349b.

4. Ibid., 634a.

5. Ibid., 617b.

6. Ibid., 236b.

7. Ibid., 204a.

8. Ibid., 219b.

CHAPTER 13.
RECONSIDERING POSSIBLE ROLES FOR ORKNEY ISLAND

1. Budge, *Egyptian Hieroglyphic Dictionary*, 318b.

2. Anonymous, *Historical and Descriptive Account*, 304–9.

3. Ibid., 310.

4. Budge, *Egyptian Hieroglyphic Dictionary*, 238a.

5. Ibid., 237b.

6. Ibid., 16a.

7. Ibid., 16a.

8. Ibid., 15b–16a.

9. Ibid., 269a.

10. Ibid., 375a.

11. Ibid., 375b.

CHAPTER 14.
THE EMERGENCE OF DYNASTIC EGYPT

1. Budge, *Egyptian Hieroglyphic Dictionary*, 783a.

2. Ibid.

3. Ibid., 782b.

4. Ibid., 947a.

5. Ibid., 19b.

6. Ibid., 18b.

7. Ibid., 947b.

8. Sauneron, *Priests of Ancient Egypt*, 173.

9. Budge, *Egyptian Hieroglyphic Dictionary*, 612a.

10. Shafer, *Temples of Ancient Egypt*, 4–5.

11. Budge, *Egyptian Hieroglyphic Dictionary*, 58b.

12. Wilkinson, *Early Dynastic Egypt*, 230.

13. Budge, *Egyptian Hieroglyphic Dictionary*, 190a.

14. Ibid., 189b.

15. Kemp, *Ancient Egypt*, 31–32.

16. Budge, *Egyptian Hieroglyphic Dictionary*, 189b.

17. Redford, *Ancient Gods Speak*, 275–76.

18. Budge, *Egyptian Hieroglyphic Dictionary*, 189b.

19. Ibid., 190a.

20. Quirke, *Ancient Egyptian Religion*, 54.

21. Budge, *Egyptian Hieroglyphic Dictionary*, 554b.

22. Ibid., 554ab.

23. Ibid., 51a.

24. Ibid., 53b.

25. Ibid., 54–55.

26. Parker, *Webster's Faroese-English Thesaurus Dictionary*, 194b.

27. Quirke, *Ancient Egyptian Religion*, 57.

CHAPTER 15. THE ADVENT OF
THE EGYPTIAN HIEROGLYPHS

1. Budge, *Egyptian Hieroglyphic Dictionary*, 6a.
2. Ibid., 800b.
3. Ibid.

CHAPTER 16.
CORRELATING REGIONAL KINGSHIPS AT 3000 BCE

1. Budge, *Egyptian Hieroglyphic Dictionary*, 653a.
2. Ibid., 21b.
3. Ibid.
4. Fantoman400, "Runic Symbols at Skara Brae and Related Sites" (jpeg), *Wikimedia Commons*, https://commons.wikimedia.org/wiki/File:Skara _Brae_symbols1.jpg (accessed May 4, 2016).
5. Budge, *Egyptian Hieroglyphic Dictionary*, 419b.
6. Ibid., 21b.
7. Ibid., 469b.
8. Quirke, *Ancient Egyptian Religion*, 54.
9. Heyerdahl, *Pyramids of Tucume*, 58–59.
10. Budge, *Egyptian Hieroglyphic Dictionary*, 243a.
11. Ibid., 29a, 576a, 1035.

CHAPTER 17.
SESHAT AND THE EGYPTIAN HOUSE OF LIFE

1. Sauneron, *Priests of Ancient Egypt*, 132–33.
2. Ibid., 136.
3. Quirke, *Ancient Egyptian Religion*, 101.
4. Budge, *Egyptian Hieroglyphic Dictionary*, 698a.
5. Hart, *Dictionary of Egyptian Gods and Goddesses*, 193.
6. Budge, *Egyptian Hieroglyphic Dictionary*, 697b.
7. Ibid., 620b.
8. Ibid., 619ab.
9. Kemp, *Ancient Egypt*, 93.
10. Ibid., 95.

11. Calame-Griaule, *Dictionnaire Dogon,* 243.

12. Ibid., 240.

13. Aldred, *Egyptians,* 36.

14. Budge, *Egyptian Hieroglyphic Dictionary,* 697b.

CHAPTER 18.
VIEWS ON THE PAPAE AND THE PETI

1. Barry, *History of the Orkney Islands,* 106.

2. Rawlinson, *History of Herodotus,* bk. II, 92.

3. Budge, *Egyptian Hieroglyphic Dictionary,* 253b.

4. Ibid., 374b.

5. Ibid., 375a.

6. Ibid., 514b.

7. Parker, *Webster's Faroese-English Thesaurus Dictionary,* 120b.

8. Ritchie, *Picts,* 5.

9. Ibid.

CHAPTER 19.
WORDS OF THE SCOTTISH GAELIC LANGUAGE

1. Campbell, "Were the Scots Irish?," 1.

2. MacBain, *Etymological Dictionary of Scottish-Gaelic,* i.

3. Ibid., 21.

4. Ibid., 303.

5. Ibid., 275, 366.

6. Ibid., 311.

7. Ibid., 302.

8. Ibid., 264.

9. Ibid., 280.

10. Ibid., 240.

11. Ibid., 240, 244.

12. Ibid., 156.

13. Ibid., 154.

CHAPTER 20.
THE DRUIDS AND OTHER PIECES OF THE PUZZLE

1. Smith, "Before Stonehenge," 49.
2. Ibid.
3. Budge, *Egyptian Hieroglyphic Dictionary,* 632a, 719b.
4. Smith, "Before Stonehenge," 49.
5. Budge, *Egyptian Hieroglyphic Dictionary,* 624b.
6. Ibid., 69a.
7. Ibid., 131b.
8. Ibid., 871b.
9. Ibid., 872a.
10. Ibid.
11. Ibid., 819b.
12. Ibid., 823b.
13. MacBain, *Etymological Dictionary of Scottish-Gaelic,* 359.
14. Budge, *Egyptian Hieroglyphic Dictionary,* 693b–694a.
15. MacBain, *Etymological Dictionary of Scottish-Gaelic,* 144.
16. Ibid., 141.
17. Healy, *Insula Sanctorum et Doctorum,* 2.
18. Ibid., 1–2.
19. Ibid., 2.
20. Calame-Griaule, *Dictionnaire Dogon,* 14–15.
21. Budge, *Egyptian Hieroglyphic Dictionary,* 113b.
22. Ibid., 516b.
23. Parker, *Webster's Faroese-English Thesaurus Dictionary,* 123a.
24. Budge, *Egyptian Hieroglyphic Dictionary,* 635a.
25. Ibid., 649b.

CHAPTER 21.
THE HINDU PARABLE OF THE SEVEN HOUSES

1. Sharma, *Devi Puran,* 16.
2. Budge, *Egyptian Hieroglyphic Dictionary,* 1b.
3. Calame-Griaule, *Dictionnaire Dogon,* 118.
4. Budge, *Egyptian Hieroglyphic Dictionary,* 28b.
5. Ibid., 620b–621a.

6. Ibid., 19b.

7. Ibid., 700b.

8. Ibid., 230a.

9. Ibid., 230b–231a.

10. Ibid., 254b.

11. Ibid., 3a.

12. Ibid., 383a.

13. Ibid., 380a.

14. Ibid., 381a.

15. Ibid., 383a.

16. Ibid., 379b.

17. Ibid., 382b.

18. Ibid., 380b.

19. Snodgrass, *Symbolism of the Stupa,* 270–71.

CHAPTER 22.
THE EGYPTIAN TALE OF THE SEVEN HOUSES
OF THE OTHER WORLD

1. Ellis, *Awakening Osiris,* ch. 9.

2. Budge, *Egyptian Hieroglyphic Dictionary,* 679b.

3. Scranton, *Sacred Symbols of the Dogon,* 139–41.

4. Budge, *Egyptian Hieroglyphic Dictionary,* 419b.

5. Ibid., 69b.

6. Ibid., 130b.

7. Ibid., 618a.

8. Ibid., 493a.

9. Ibid., 163b.

10. Ibid., 274a.

11. Ibid., 15a, 17b.

12. Ibid., 14a.

13. Ibid., 377b.

14. Ibid., 377a.

15. Ibid., 67a.

16. Ibid., 107a.

17. Ibid., 137b.

18. Ibid., 398b.

19. Ibid., 375a.

20. Ibid., 617b.

21. Ibid., 397b.

22. Ibid.

23. Ibid., 669b.

24. Ibid., 667b.

25. Ibid., 174b.

26. Ibid., 150a.

27. Ibid., 151a.

28. Ibid., 843a.

29. Ibid., 412a.

30. Ibid., 335b.

31. Ibid., 711a.

32. Ibid., 773a.

33. Ibid., 729a.

34. Ibid., 23a.

35. Ibid., 37b.

36. Ibid., 3a.

37. Ibid., 37b.

38. Ibid., 55a.

39. Ibid., 38b.

40. Ibid., 554a.

41. Ibid., 129a.

42. Ibid., 360a.

43. Ibid., 529a.

44. Ibid., 326a.

45. Ibid., 224b.

46. Ibid., 206a.

47. Ibid., 135a.

48. Ibid., 424b, 425b.

49. Ibid., 425a.

50. Ibid., 734–36.

51. Ibid., 23b.

52. Ibid., 16b

53. Ibid., 908b.

54. Ibid., 37a.

55. Ibid., 5a.

56. Ibid., 619–20.

57. Ibid., 428b–429a.

58. Ibid., 83a.

59. Ibid., 29a.

60. Ibid., 72a.

61. Ibid., 474b, 476a.

62. Ibid., 400a.

63. Ibid., 382a.

64. Ibid., 115b.

65. Ibid., 4a.

66. Ibid., 2b.

67. Ibid., 3b.

68. Ibid., 355b.

69. Ibid., 355a.

70. Ibid., 6b.

71. Ibid., 694a.

72. Ibid., 693b.

73. Ibid., 214a.

74. Ibid., 468a.

75. Ibid., 220a.

76. Ibid., 154b.

77. Ibid.

78. Ibid., 165a.

79. Ibid., 154a.

80. Ibid., 385b.

81. Ibid., 636b.

82. Ibid.

83. Ibid., 548a.

84. Ibid.

85. Ibid., 291b.

86. Ibid., 83a.

CHAPTER 23.
CONCLUSIONS AND OBSERVATIONS

1. Kemp, *Ancient Egypt,* 37.
2. Ibid.
3. Budge, *Egyptian Hieroglyphic Dictionary,* 238a.

BIBLIOGRAPHY

Aldred, Cyril. *The Egyptians*. Revised ed. London: Thames and Hudson, 1984.

Anonymous. *An Historical and Descriptive Account of Iceland, Greenland, and the Faroe Islands; with Illustrations of Their Natural History*. 5th ed. Edinburgh: Oliver & Boyd, 1840.

Arnold, Caroline. *Stone Age Farmers beside the Sea: Scotland's Prehistoric Village of Skara Brae*. New York: Clarion Books, 1997.

Barnes, Michael P. *The Norn Language of Orkney and Shetland*. Lerwick, Scotland: Shetland Times, Ltd., 1998.

Barry, George. *History of the Orkney Islands*. London: Printed for Longman, Hurst, Rees, and Orme, Paternoster-Row, 1808.

BBC. "Scotland's History: Skara Brae." www.bbc.co.uk/scotland/history/articles /skara_brae (accessed May 2, 2016).

Budge, E. A. Wallis. *An Egyptian Hieroglyphic Dictionary*. New York: Dover Publications, Inc., 1978.

Calame-Griaule, Genevieve. *Dictionnaire Dogon*. Paris: Librarie C. Klincksieck, 1968.

Campbell, Ewan. "Were the Scots Irish?" *Antiquity* 75 (2001): 295–92.

Cenival, Jean-Louis de, and Geneviève Pierrat-Bonnefois. "Fragment of the *Book of the Dead* on Papyrus: Djedhor Working in the Fields of the Afterlife." Louvre. www.louvre.fr/en/oeuvre-notices/fragment-book-dead-papyrus-djedhor-working-fields-afterlife (accessed May 2, 2016).

Childe, V. Gordon, and D. V. Clarke. *Skara Brae*. Edinburgh: Her Majesty's Stationery Office (HMSO), 1983.

Clark, Katharine. *An Irish Book of Shadows: Tuatha de Danaan*. Lakeville, Minn.: Galde Press, 2011.

Dunrea, Olivier. *Skara Brae: The Story of a Prehistoric Village*. New York: Holiday House, 1985.

Ellis, Normandi. *Awakening Osiris: The Egyptian Book of the Dead*. Grand Rapids, Mich.: Phanes Press, 1988.

Frankfort, Henri. *Ancient Egyptian Religion*. New York: Columbia University Press, 1948.

Griaule, Marcel. *Conversations with Ogotemmeli*. Oxford: Oxford University Press, 1970.

Griaule, Marcel, and Germaine Dieterlen. *The Pale Fox*. Paris: Continuum Foundation, 1986.

Hart, George. *A Dictionary of Egyptian Gods and Goddesses*. London and New York: Routledge, 1999.

Healy, John. *Insula Sanctorum et Doctorum; or Ireland's Ancients Schools and Scholars*. Dublin: Sealy, Bryers & Walker, 1897.

Heyerdahl, Thor. *Pyramids of Tucume: The Quest for Peru's Forgotten City*. New York: Thames and Hudson, 1995.

Hibbert, Samuel, M.D. *A Description of the Shetland Islands, Comprising an Account of Their Scenery, Antiquities, and Superstitions*. Lerwick, Scotland: T. & J. Manson, 1891.

Higgins, Charlotte. "Scottish People's DNA Study Could 'Rewrite Nation's History.'" *Guardian,* August 15, 2012. www.theguardian.com/uk/2012/aug/15/scotland-dna-study-project (accessed May 2, 2016).

Horowitz, Edward. *How the Hebrew Language Grew*. Brooklyn, N.Y.: KTAV Publishing House, Inc., 1960.

Kemp, Barry J. *Ancient Egypt: Anatomy of a Civilization*. London and New York: Routledge, 1989.

Lewis, A. L. "The Stone Circles of Scotland." *Journal of the Anthropological Institute of Great Britain and Ireland* 30 (1900). http://goo.gl/fgjuek.

MacBain, Alexander. *Etymological Dictionary of Scottish-Gaelic*. New York: Hippocrene Books, 1998.

Mann, Allison. "Vikings, Merchants, and Pirates at the Top of the World: Y-chromosomal Signatures of Recent and Ancient Migrations in the Faroe Islands." *Electronic Theses and Dissertations*. Paper 901 (2012). http://dx.doi.org/10.18297/etd/901 (accessed June 15, 2016).

Miller, D. Gary. *External Influences on English: From Its Beginnings to the Renaissance*. Oxford: Oxford University Press, 2012.

Miller, Joyce. *Myth and Magic: Scotland's Ancient Beliefs and Sacred Ancient Places.* Musselburgh, Scotland: Goblinshead, 2000.

National Library of Scotland. *Blaeu Atlas of Scotland.* 1654. http://maps.nls.uk /atlas/blaeu/place/o.html (accessed May 2, 2016).

Orkneyjar: The Heritage of the Orkney Islands. "The Climate of Orkney." www .orkneyjar.com/orkney/climate.htm (accessed May 2, 2016).

Parker, Philip M., ed. *Webster's Faroese-English Thesaurus Dictionary.* San Diego, Calif.: ICON Classics, 2008.

Pontikos, Dienekes. Dienekes Anthropology Blog. dienekes.blogspot.com (accessed September 15, 2016).

Pritchard, James B., ed. *Ancient Near-Eastern Texts Relating to the Old Testament.* 3rd ed. with suppl. Princeton, N.J.: Princeton University Press, 1969.

Quirke, Stephen. *Ancient Egyptian Religion.* London: British Museum Press, 1992.

Rawlinson, George, trans. *The History of Herodotus.* New York: Tudor Publishing Company, 1934.

Redford, Donald B., ed. *The Ancient Gods Speak: A Guide to Egyptian Religion.* Oxford: Oxford University Press, 2002.

Renton, R. W., and J. A. MacDonald. *Scottish Gaelic–English/English–Scottish Gaelic Dictionary.* New York: Hippocrene Books, 1994.

Rice, Michael. *Egypt's Making: The Origins of Ancient Egypt 5000–2000 BC.* New York: Routledge, 1990.

Richards, Colin, ed. *Building the Great Stone Circles of the North.* Oxford: Oxbow Books, 2013.

Ritchie, Anna. *Pictish Carved Stones.* Edinburgh: Historic Scotland, 1997.

———. *Picts: An Introduction to the Life of the Picts and the Carved Stones in the Care of the Secretary of State for Scotland.* Edinburgh: Her Majesty's Stationery Office (HMSO), 1989.

———. *Scotland BC.* Edinburgh: Her Majesty's Stationery Office (HMSO), 1988.

Sauneron, Serge. *The Priests of Ancient Egypt.* New ed. Ithaca, N.Y.: Cornell University Press, 2000.

Schoenauer, Norbert. *6,000 Years of Housing.* New York: W. W. Norton, 1981.

Scranton, Laird. *The Cosmological Origins of Myth and Symbol: From the Dogon and Ancient Egypt to India, Tibet, and China.* Rochester, Vt.: Inner Traditions, 2010.

———. *Sacred Symbols of the Dogon: The Key to Advanced Science in the Ancient Egyptian Hieroglyphics.* Rochester, Vt.: Inner Traditions, 2007.

———. *The Science of the Dogon: Decoding the African Mystery Tradition.* Rochester, Vt.: Inner Traditions, 2007.

Shafer, Byron E. *Temples of Ancient Egypt.* Ithaca, N.Y.: Cornell University Press, 1997.

Sharma, Janaky. *Devi Puran.* Chandigarh, India: Abhishek Publications, 2009.

Smith, Roff. "Before Stonehenge." *National Geographic,* August 2014, 27–51.

Snodgrass, Adrian. *The Symbolism of the Stupa.* Delhi, India: Motilal Banarsidass Publishers, 1992.

Theoi Greek Mythology. "Realm of Elysion." www.theoi.com/Kosmos/Elysion .html (accessed May 2, 2016).

Thornhill, Ted. "'Discovery of a Lifetime': Stone Age Temple Found in Orkney Is 800 Years Older than Stonehenge— and May Be More Important." *Daily Mail,* January 2, 2012. www.dailymail.co.uk/sciencetech/article-2081254/Stone-Age -temple-Orkney-significant-Stonehenge.html (accessed May 2, 2016).

Wilkinson, Toby A. H. *Early Dynastic Egypt.* New York: Routledge, 1999.

Woodlief, Ann. "The Story of Orpheus and Eurydice, as Told by Apollonius of Rhodes, Virgil, and Ovid (and Retold by Edith Hamilton in *Mythology*)." English Department, Virginia Commonwealth University. www.vcu.edu /engweb/webtexts/eurydice/eurydicemyth.html (accessed May 2, 2016).

Wood-Martin, W. G., M.R.I.A. *Traces of the Elder Faiths of Ireland.* London: Longmans, Green and Co., 1902.

Wylie, Jonathan, and David Margolin. *The Ring of Dancers: Images of Faroese Culture.* Philadelphia: University of Pennsylvania Press, 1981.

INDEX

BOOKS OF RELATED INTEREST

Point of Origin
Gobekli Tepe and the Spiritual Matrix for the World's Cosmologies
by Laird Scranton

The Science of the Dogon
Decoding the African Mystery Tradition
by Laird Scranton
Foreword by John Anthony West

Sacred Symbols of the Dogon
The Key to Advanced Science in the Ancient Egyptian Hieroglyphs
by Laird Scranton
Foreword by John Anthony West

The Velikovsky Heresies
Worlds in Collision and Ancient Catastrophes Revisited
by Laird Scranton

The Great Pyramid Hoax
The Conspiracy to Conceal the True History of Ancient Egypt
by Scott Creighton
Foreword by Laird Scranton

Göbekli Tepe: Genesis of the Gods
The Temple of the Watchers and the Discovery of Eden
by Andrew Collins
Introduction by Graham Hancock

Black Genesis
The Prehistoric Origins of Ancient Egypt
by Robert Bauval and Thomas Brophy, Ph.D.

Forgotten Civilization
The Role of Solar Outbursts in Our Past and Future
by Robert M. Schoch, Ph.D.

INNER TRADITIONS • BEAR & COMPANY
P.O. Box 388
Rochester, VT 05767
1-800-246-8648
www.InnerTraditions.com

Or contact your local bookseller